2007.

Dearest Kate
Merry Christmas.
with much love.
Mum and Pops. xx

A Year of Family Recipes

LESLEY WILD

Bettys Café Tea Rooms;
Parliament Street, Harrogate
RHS Garden Harlow Carr, Harrogate
St Helen's Square, York
Stonegate, York
The Grove, Ilkley
High Street, Northallerton
www.bettysandtaylors.co.uk

**To find out more about Bettys Cookery School
or to order specialist equipment from our Cookshop
please telephone 01423 814016 or visit our website at
www.bettyscookeryschool.co.uk**

This book is for my children Chloë and Daniel.

I hope that they will enjoy using the recipes
and pass them on to their own families and friends.

Writing and producing this book has taken just over a year – a year of pure pleasure for me, working with a small but hugely talented team.

My special thanks go to Head Designer, Rebecca, and Stylist Georgina, who have so enthusiastically dedicated more than twelve months of their lives to this project. From the outset they understood my vision for the book and were able to make it a reality – we have not quibbled over a single detail.

My grateful thanks also go to:

Sue and her assistants Rhonda and Georgina, who made photography in my home so painless and the food look so beautiful. Also, Sandra and Elaine for coping with so much washing up and returning our house to normality after photography sessions.

The Cookery School team for their steadfast support and assistance – Richard, Amy and Roxy who helped prepare the dishes in my kitchen; Lisa who tried and tested recipes at the Cookery School; Mary, Emma, Dawn, Maggie and Tirath who have helped and encouraged me in so many ways.

John and Mr Blackie Senior for all their hard work in our garden over the years.

Mr and Mrs Naish for their kind interest and for supplying some of the 'wilder' ingredients.

All those who have shared their knowledge, expertise and recipes with me – particularly my mother, my father-in-law Victor, my sister Lyn and chef Corrado Corti in Portofino.

This is also the most appropriate place to thank my parents who have instilled in me a love of producing, cooking and enjoying good food – especially my mother, who always encouraged me to help her in the kitchen and has taught me so well.

My final thanks go to my family for their support through the process of writing this book – particularly to Jonathan, for supplying me with the most beautiful vegetables and fruit.

Contents

A Consuming Passion

There is a story behind this book – in many ways it's the story of my life. I am not a chef, just a simple cook and, as a child, certainly never imagined that I would have a culinary career. And yet, looking back over my early years, it now seems inevitable that with my background I would develop a passion for cooking.

Good food has always been of the utmost importance in our family – not just the love of eating it, but also the pleasure of producing it. Both of my parents have farming in their blood. My paternal grandfather's family owned a large vegetable garden, which supplied them with produce for their village shop. In his turn my father had a farm in the Yorkshire Wolds, high above the town in which we lived.

My Irish mother was the daughter of a sheep farmer who strayed from her roots to embark on a career in catering, settled in Yorkshire and married my father in 1951. The same vegetable garden that had provided an income for my grandparents' generation became my parents' kitchen garden supplying their growing family with fresh fruit and vegetables.

Seasonality, the theme of this book, and currently the fashionable way to eat, was simply the way we lived, there was no alternative. We were in touch with the rhythm of the year and eagerly anticipated the arrival of each vegetable and fruit as it became available. Preserving food for consumption during

Me as a child

My parents on holiday
in the South of France

the winter was a challenge. Hams were cured and hung in our pantry, huge stoneware crocks were filled with eggs and waterglass – hens had a winter break in those days. Root vegetables were gathered into piles and covered with earth, and apples were stored on trays in our outhouse. The pantry shelves were lined with jars of jam and bottled fruit. I remember well the arrival of our first freezer, allowing us to enjoy fresh garden peas, beans and soft fruit through the winter for the first time.

There was always a delicious meal on the table; my mother was, and still is, a superb cook. I loved to help her in the kitchen – on baking days I was in heaven. We made cakes, biscuits, meringues and fruit pies, all of which were stored away in tins in the pantry. I gradually progressed to making puddings for Sunday lunch and helping to freeze the glut of fresh fruit and vegetables from the garden. At school I was considered too bright for cookery lessons. However, I now realise I had the best of all home tutors.

My father was particularly fussy about his meat – he regularly experimented in his quest to cook his steak to perfection; he liked it charred on the outside and rare on the inside. On one memorable occasion he held the grill pan too close to the flames of the grill; dramatically the fat in the pan caught fire. With one deft movement, he threw the flaming grill pan through the open kitchen window whilst stabbing the steak with a fork, and sat down triumphantly at the table to enjoy his lunch, leaving the kitchen curtains blazing.

Home-grown ingredients were supplemented from time to time with game shot by my father or fish from the east coast. Most Sunday afternoons, after a proper Sunday lunch and dressed in our Sunday best, we drove over the Wolds to Scarborough. Our jaunts invariably concluded with a stroll round the harbour where the pick of the catch was purchased, followed by afternoon tea in a posh hotel with a pianist.

This 'hunter-gatherer' instinct could not be suppressed, even on holiday in the South of France. Leaving the rest of the family to enjoy the beach, my father would spend his time at the local market, returning to our rented flat laden with cases of exotic fruit and vegetables, an array of ripe pungent cheeses and even, on one occasion, a live chicken.

Fast forward to the early seventies when nine or ten years later, I went on my first proper date with Jonathan. He was a history undergraduate at Oxford, I was an Art College student in York. We had met several years earlier at the house of a mutual friend. He invited me to a hog roast at his college which he was helping to organise, so I drove to Oxford for the weekend. When I arrived I found him looking rather panic stricken. "Are you any good at making potato salad?" he asked. I spent the rest of the afternoon in the basement kitchens slicing potatoes and mixing them with mayonnaise in huge bowls. Looking back, this was a pivotal

The hog roast! Oxford 1971

Jonathan and me as students
Oxford 1973

Afternoon tea at Bettys

Demonstrating at
Bettys Cookery School

moment in our relationship – I had proved myself both in the kitchen and as a willing assistant. Just over four years later we were married.

Five days before our wedding, Jonathan had joined his family's business, Bettys & Taylors. We had a three-day honeymoon and then he was back at work. It was inevitable that I would be drawn into this world of tea shops, but I resisted. First I helped out unpaid whilst I qualified as a solicitor and completed a textile course. Not too many years later I was running the Bettys side of the business whilst Jonathan concentrated his energies on the tea and coffee importing business. The culinary training instilled in me by my parents was invaluable. I loved every aspect of Bettys, from designing bread, cakes and menu dishes to café décor and waitresses' uniforms. Life was good, and of course we had our own vegetable garden at home.

Then in 2001, my dreams came true. We had acquired more land in Harrogate to build a new Craft Bakery, and before Jonathan had time to demolish a redundant building in the corner of the site, I had refurbished it and opened the doors of Bettys Cookery School for business. It is my own part of Bettys where we train all our cooks; where our master bakers, chocolatiers, confectioners and cooks can share their skills with others; and above all a place that I can offer as a free facility to local schools in an attempt, in some small way, to compensate for the lack of practical cooking skills in the national curriculum. In the last six years, Bettys

Cookery School has gone from strength to strength, with its training kitchen and specialist cookshop busy every day of the week. We have even started to grow our own vegetables in the garden at the back.

This book is about the way I cook at home for my family and friends. I have collected and developed the recipes over many years. Some have been handed down to me by my mother and Swiss father-in-law. Others are based on food I have enjoyed whilst travelling abroad.

Every dish has been made in my own kitchen, photographed with all its imperfections in our house or garden and eaten at the end of each photography session by the photographers and my Cookery School helpers. It has taken a full year to write as I waited for the right moment to use the fruit and vegetables that Jonathan and I grow in our garden. Eating seasonally ensures that you use the freshest and best-quality ingredients. That is what I learned as a child and what I want to share with you in this book.

A family meal in our garden

Happy, joyous cooking!
Lesley

The Garden

Whilst I am perfectly at home in the kitchen, Jonathan is a natural in the garden. When he was a small child, his family home had enormous grounds with a large greenhouse. He can still remember the delicious sensation of eating ripe home-grown peaches for breakfast.

As soon as we moved into our first marital home in Tockwith, North Yorkshire, we started a small kitchen garden. Luckily our neighbours, Norman and Elsie Brogden, were also keen vegetable growers and conscientiously coached Jonathan through the seasons. Quickly he learned that Boxing Day was the time to sow onion seeds and Good Friday the day on which to plant seed potatoes. The only advice we questioned was Norman's insistence that watering carrots with Jeyes Fluid was a sure way of combating carrot root fly – the carrots were inedible! Seven years later, Jonathan had become so proficient in the garden that he was asked to become Horticultural Secretary of the Tockwith Show – the youngest secretary in the show's history.

With the arrival of our first baby, we moved to Harrogate. We couldn't believe our luck; we had found a house close to the town centre with two-thirds of an acre of garden. Immediately Jonathan set about converting a rather run-down ornamental rose garden into a potager where he grew all our vegetables. We planted apple, pear and plum trees around the base of our south-facing terrace – but we still hankered after a little more space. We never imagined in our wildest dreams that twenty years later we would acquire a large plot of land adjoining our existing garden. Now, with our own acre and a new greenhouse, we can grow everything we need to be self-sufficient.

I could not have written this book without Jonathan's invaluable contribution. Last spring, when I hesitantly gave him the list of almost 60 different ingredients that I needed for the recipes, he enthusiastically set to work and provided me with every one. His beautiful vegetables and fruit are the stars of the recipes in this book.

Spring

Recipes

Seville Orange Marmalade

The bitter oranges which are traditionally used to make marmalade come from Seville, the capital of the southern Spanish province of Andalucía. Although orange trees line the peaceful squares of the city, they are not for sale in the local shops – they are 'free food' – available to anyone who wants to pick them. As the Spaniards are not particularly partial to marmalade, the bulk of the crop is exported to Britain. As the peel of the oranges is part of the recipe, use organic fruit if possible. This recipe came with the oranges – from Seville itself.

Method

1. Wash the oranges and cut in half. With a small sharp knife, remove the pips and reserve. Squeeze the halved oranges and set the juice to one side. Add the lemon juice to the orange juice.

2. Scrape any remaining flesh from the orange halves and discard. Slice the peel finely. Place the reserved pips on a square of muslin – these help to set the marmalade. Draw together the corners and tie tightly with string.

3. Place the water, orange and lemon juice, pips and peel in a large, heavy-based saucepan or preserve pan and leave to steep in a cool place for at least 24 hours.

4. After steeping, transfer the uncovered pan to the stove and bring the contents to the boil. Continue to simmer until the peel is soft – this will take 1 - 1½ hours, depending on the size of the pieces of peel. The liquid should be considerably reduced at this stage. Remove from the heat and leave to cool for a few minutes. Lift out the pips tied in muslin and discard.

5. Preheat the oven to 180°C (gas mark 4). Sterilise your jam jars and lids by washing them in hot soapy water, then rinsing – do not dry them with a tea towel. Place in the oven for at least 10 minutes, then remove and allow to cool slightly.

Ingredients

Makes 5 - 6 small jars

700g Seville oranges

juice of 1 lemon

2.2 litres water

approximately 1½kg granulated sugar

Seville Orange Marmalade

6. When the liquid is cool enough to handle, pour it from the pan into a measuring jug to calculate how much liquid you have. You will need one pound of sugar for every pint of liquid – 450g of sugar per 570ml of liquid.

7. Return the liquid to the pan with the peel. Add the appropriate amount of sugar. Place over a low heat, stirring well until the sugar has dissolved completely. Bring to the boil and cook rapidly until setting point is reached – this could take as long as 20 - 40 minutes, depending on the acidity of the oranges and the shape of your pan. To test for setting point, place a saucer in the fridge to cool. Spoon a small amount of marmalade onto the cold saucer and return to the fridge for a moment or two. The marmalade will be ready if it wrinkles when you push it with your finger.

8. Remove the pan from the heat. It is very important to let the marmalade stand for 20 minutes before transferring it to the jam jars – if you are too hasty, the peel will not be evenly distributed throughout the marmalade.

9. Pour the marmalade into the sterilised jam jars and cover the surface with a waxed disc, wax side down. Seal with lids whilst still hot to allow a vacuum to form. Allow to cool for 24 hours before labelling and storing in a cool, dark place.

SEVILLE ORANGES

Seville oranges are a truly seasonal crop. They are harvested in January and have all but disappeared from our shops by the end of February. The flesh is extremely tart and full of pips – perfect for preserve-making because of its high acid content.

Twice-baked Spinach & Gruyère Soufflés

These individual soufflés make a delicious starter or a wonderfully light main course served with fresh new potatoes. They can be made up to 24 hours ahead, kept in the fridge and finished off at the last minute.

Method

1. Butter 10 - 12 individual ovenproof ramekins or dariole moulds with a little of the butter. Preheat the oven to 180°C (gas mark 4). Place the spinach into a heavy-based pan with the milk. Bring to the boil and set aside.

2. In a second saucepan, melt the butter and add the flour. Cook for a couple of minutes over a low heat, stirring well. Remove from the heat and gradually add the milk and spinach, stirring until smooth. Return to the heat and keep stirring until the sauce thickens. Remove from the heat again, cool slightly, then add the salt, pepper, nutmeg and Gruyère, followed by the egg yolks and stir well.

3. In a large clean mixing bowl whisk the egg whites until they form peaks, then carefully fold into the cheese mixture with a metal spoon, a little at a time. Transfer to the prepared ramekins or moulds – each should be two-thirds full. Arrange them in a deep metal tray then pour boiling water around them until it comes halfway up the sides of the ramekins.

4. Place in the preheated oven and bake for 20 - 25 minutes, until set and springy to the touch. Remove from the oven, lift the ramekins carefully out of the water and allow to cool.

5. Butter a large ovenproof serving dish and sprinkle with half the Parmesan cheese. Run a knife round the soufflés to loosen them. Turn them out of the ramekins and place upside down in the dish. This is the point at which the soufflés can be refrigerated for up to 24 hours.

Ingredients

Makes approximately 10

125g small-leaf spinach, washed with any tough stalks removed, shredded finely

300ml semi-skimmed milk

70g butter

55g plain white flour

salt & freshly ground black pepper

a scraping of freshly grated nutmeg

75g Gruyère cheese, grated

4 large eggs, separated

75g Parmesan cheese, freshly grated

400ml double cream

2 tablespoons fresh chives, finely chopped

Twice-baked Spinach & Gruyère Soufflés

CHIVES

One of the first herbs to appear in the garden in spring, chives have a delicate onion flavour. Chop finely with a sharp knife and use to garnish soups, salads, stews and buttered new potatoes.

EGGS

Eggs should be stored in a cool place and returned to room temperature before use. The freshest eggs have a thick viscous white and a firm, domed yolk, which varies in colour according to the diet of the hen.

6. Preheat the oven to 220°C (gas mark 7). To finish the dish, season the cream with salt and freshly ground black pepper and pour over the soufflés, coating them completely. Finally, sprinkle them with the remaining Parmesan cheese and place in the oven for 10 – 15 minutes until risen and golden. Scatter with chives and serve immediately.

18

Watercress Soup

Watercress has a delicious peppery flavour and is packed full of vitamins. It is an interesting and tasty addition to salads, and also makes a beautiful, rich-green nutritious soup. The potatoes are included to thicken the soup, so use a floury variety such as 'King Edward'.

Method

1. Melt the butter in a large, heavy-based saucepan, add the onion and cook gently for several minutes until soft but not browned.

2. Add the potatoes, milk and seasonings and bring slowly to the boil. Simmer until the potatoes are tender – approximately 10 minutes.

3. Whilst the potatoes and onion are simmering, trim the watercress, discarding any coarse stalks. Reserve a few sprigs for garnishing, then roughly chop the rest.

4. Once the potatoes are cooked, add the watercress and cook for a further 2 - 3 minutes. Take care, the watercress will discolour if it is kept too long over the heat.

5. Allow to cool slightly, then purée using an electric hand blender, liquidiser or food processor.

6. To serve, reheat gently and adjust the seasoning. Garnish each portion with a sprig of the reserved watercress.

Ingredients

Serves 6

200g watercress

50g butter

1 medium onion, finely chopped

2 medium to large potatoes, peeled and diced

1 litre semi-skimmed milk

salt & freshly ground black pepper

WATERCRESS

Prized by Hippocrates for its health-giving properties, watercress is a valuable source of vitamins C, A and K, potassium, iron, calcium and copper. As the name suggests, it is grown in flowing water.

Pork & Herb Terrine

Serve this delicious rustic terrine as a starter with crusty bread, or as a light main course with a leafy side salad.

Method

1. Preheat the oven to 160°C (gas mark 2½). Put the spinach leaves in a large, heavy-based saucepan and place over a moderate heat. Stir well as they wilt in their own juices. When completely softened, remove from the pan and drain in a large sieve or colander. Press well to squeeze out all the liquid. When cool, chop roughly and set aside.

2. Melt the butter in a small, heavy-based saucepan over a moderate heat. Add the onion and garlic. Cook for a few minutes, stirring occasionally until they are soft but not coloured. Remove from the heat and allow to cool.

3. Place the liver and both types of bacon in a food processor and pulse until finely chopped. Add the minced pork, spinach, softened onion and garlic, herbs, nutmeg, salt and freshly ground black pepper. Process a little longer until all the ingredients are amalgamated together. Finally, mix in the lightly beaten egg.

4. Grease a terrine mould or loaf tin with a little butter, then fill with the terrine mixture. Cover with the lid or tin foil and bake in the preheated oven for approximately 50 minutes. Remove the lid or foil and leave in the oven for a further 10 - 15 minutes to brown the top. Leave to cool completely before serving.

Ingredients

Makes one terrine, approximately 24 x 7 x 6cm deep
Serves 10

- 350g fresh spinach leaves, with any tough stalks removed, washed and dried
- 25g butter
- 1 medium onion, chopped very finely
- 1 large garlic clove, chopped or crushed
- 125g pigs liver
- 50g smoked lean bacon
- 50g streaky bacon
- 500g minced pork
- 1 tablespoon fresh rosemary, chopped
- 3 or 4 sprigs of fresh thyme, finely chopped
- 1 tablespoon fresh basil, chopped
- a generous scraping of freshly grated nutmeg
- salt & freshly ground black pepper
- 1 egg, lightly beaten

Broccoli, Chive & Parmesan Frittata

This dish is a wonderful combination of all that is new, fresh and best in spring – eggs, sprouting broccoli and tender young chives. The Italian version of an omelette, a frittata is flat and quite solid in texture. This recipe will make a large frittata which can be shared between 3 or 4 people.

Method

1. Trim and wash the broccoli, then chop into small pieces approximately 1cm in length.

2. Crack the eggs into a large bowl. Add the milk, chives, Parmesan, salt and freshly ground black pepper. Beat together with a hand whisk until amalgamated. Set aside.

3. Heat the oil in a large (approximately 26cm) heavy-based non-stick frying pan. Add the garlic and the broccoli and fry over a low heat, stirring frequently until the broccoli feels tender when pierced with a knife. If the broccoli is very fresh and tender, this will only take 2 – 3 minutes. Season lightly. Preheat the grill.

4. Pour the beaten egg mixture over the broccoli, making sure it covers the whole of the bottom of the pan. Stir gently until the egg begins to set. Cook over a medium heat for 3 – 4 minutes.

5. Transfer the pan to the grill and cook for a further 2 – 3 minutes, until the top of the frittata is set and golden.

6. To serve, portion the frittata with a sharp knife, garnish the top of each slice with Parmesan shavings and serve with a fresh garden salad.

Ingredients

Serves 3 - 4

- 300g (before trimming) purple sprouting broccoli
- 8 large eggs
- 50ml semi-skimmed milk
- 2 tablespoons fresh chives, finely chopped
- 100g Parmesan cheese, freshly grated
- salt & freshly ground black pepper
- 2 tablespoons olive oil
- 1 garlic clove, crushed
- fresh Parmesan shavings

BROCCOLI

Purple sprouting broccoli is one of the first vegetables in our garden to appear in spring. To prepare as a side dish, trim off any woody stems and leaves and rinse under cold water. Bring a pan of salted water to the boil, add the broccoli and cook until just tender when pierced with a small sharp knife (3 - 4 minutes).

Lemon Chicken & Herb Salad

Fresh, organic spring chicken is succulent and tasty. In this recipe it is tenderised with a delicious spicy lemon and yoghurt marinade. The choice of salad leaves is entirely up to you, but the dish works best with small mixed leaves such as rocket, lamb's lettuce, baby chard and spinach.

Method

1. First make the marinade. Combine the lemon juice and zest, yoghurt, olive oil, garlic, coriander and cumin together in a large mixing bowl. Season with salt and freshly ground black pepper. Set aside.

2. Cut the raw chicken into 2cm-wide strips and add to the marinade, stirring the mixture well to ensure it is completely coated. Cover and leave in the fridge for at least 2 hours.

3. Preheat the grill. Cut the peppers into strips 1½cm wide, season, and place under the grill together with the strips of marinated chicken. Turn after two or three minutes and cook until the chicken juices run clear and both peppers and meat are nicely browned.

4. Meanwhile make the dressing by placing all the ingredients together in a small jug or bowl. Blend together with a hand whisk until emulsified.

5. Arrange the baby salad leaves in a salad bowl and scatter with the tomatoes, cucumber and herbs. Add the warm chicken and peppers to the bowl, together with the salad dressing. Serve immediately.

Ingredients

Serves 4

grated zest of 1 lemon and juice of 2

50ml natural yoghurt

2 teaspoons olive oil

2 garlic cloves, crushed

1 tablespoon fresh coriander, finely chopped

½ teaspoon ground cumin

salt & freshly ground black pepper

500g raw chicken breast

1 red and 1 yellow pepper

200g mixed baby salad leaves

12 baby plum tomatoes, halved

¼ of a large cucumber, chopped

1 tablespoon each of fresh dill, coriander, chives and parsley, chopped

For the dressing

6 tablespoons extra virgin olive oil

1 tablespoon freshly squeezed lemon juice

1 tablespoon white wine vinegar

½ teaspoon caster sugar

Spinach & Mozzarella Tart

I first started to make this tart over 25 years ago. In those days, mozzarella came in the form of a rubbery vacuum-packed rectangle and fresh spinach was hard to find. Soon after we moved into our first proper house with a small vegetable patch, I was putting in my order – a difficult request to fulfil, as a kilo of spinach leaves is required for this recipe. Fortunately, these days both leaf spinach and fresh mozzarella are readily available.

The light wholewheat pastry is a perfect contrast to the cheese and spinach filling. However, if you prefer, you could use simple shortcrust pastry (see recipe p233).

Method

1. First make the pastry as described on p234. Remove from the fridge and allow to almost reach room temperature. Lightly dust the work surface and rolling pin with flour, then roll the pastry out, lightly but firmly. Keep turning it and dusting the work surface to ensure it doesn't stick. The pastry needs to be larger than your flan dish and approximately 3mm thick. Wrap it around the rolling pin and lift it over the flan dish, gently pushing it down the sides. Trim off the excess with a sharp knife. Place the lined flan dish in the fridge and leave to rest for at least 20 minutes. Preheat the oven to 180°C (gas mark 4).

2. When the pastry has rested, take a piece of baking parchment slightly larger than the dish, screw it up and then flatten it out again. Place over the pastry – it should mould itself to the correct shape. Cover the base of the dish with ceramic baking beans or rice and place in the preheated oven. After 10 minutes, remove the baking parchment and beans and return the dish to the oven for a further 5 - 10 minutes, until the pastry is set and slightly coloured.

Ingredients

For a 28cm fluted flan dish
Serves 6

450g wholewheat pastry (recipe p234)

1kg fresh spinach leaves, washed with any tough stalks removed

large knob of butter

2 medium onions, finely chopped

4 garlic cloves, crushed

750g mozzarella cheese

juice of 1 lemon

freshly grated nutmeg

salt & freshly ground black pepper

SPINACH

This leafy vegetable is an excellent source of iron, vitamin C and calcium. As a side dish, wilt the leaves in a saucepan over a moderate to high heat for 3 - 4 minutes with a little salt and freshly ground black pepper. Drain off any liquid and finish with a little butter or cream and a scraping of nutmeg.

Spinach & Mozzarella Tart

BUFFALO MOZZARELLA CHEESE

Buffalo are an ancient breed, originating in the Far East. The Arabs brought them to the Middle East in early Christian times and in the Middle Ages they were introduced to Europe. There is still a sizeable population of around 100,000 in the Campania region of Italy, which supplies the rich creamy milk for the original mozzarella cheese. The photograph above, taken on a winter walking holiday, shows that a few buffalo also live in Switzerland.

3. Next, prepare the spinach. Bit by bit, add it to a large, heavy-based saucepan over a low to moderate heat. Sprinkle with salt and freshly ground black pepper. There should be no need to add water; the spinach will cook in its own juices. When thoroughly wilted, remove from the pan and place in a sieve. Lay a small plate or saucer over the top and press to squeeze all the moisture out of the spinach. Transfer to a large, clean bowl.

4. Now prepare the rest of the filling. In a small, heavy-based saucepan, soften the onions and garlic in the knob of butter over a low heat until they are translucent but not coloured. Add to the spinach in the bowl.

5. Chop the mozzarella into small cubes – roughly 1cm in size. Add to the bowl together with the lemon juice and a generous grating of fresh nutmeg. Combine all the ingredients together thoroughly, adding a little more salt and pepper.

6. Pack the filling into the pastry-lined flan dish and place in the oven for 35 – 40 minutes, until the filling is bubbling and the cheese has turned golden brown. Delicious with salad and fresh new potatoes.

Asparagus

The English asparagus season is relatively short, beginning in late April or early May, and ending on midsummer's day. It is possible to buy asparagus all year round, grown on the far side of the world and flown thousands of miles to the supermarkets. However, there is nothing to compare with the flavour of fresh, tender, succulent spears grown locally – or even better, in your own garden.

Asparagus can be served with melted butter, hollandaise sauce (see recipe p238), or cold with a dressing. My favourite recipe, however, is Asparagus with Prosciutto & Parmesan (see recipe overleaf).

To prepare asparagus

1. You will need approximately 200g of asparagus per person. Take the spears one at a time and bend the stem somewhere towards the bottom. You will find that it naturally snaps at the point at which it has become woody. Discard the snapped-off ends, and wash the remaining stems in cold water.

2. Choose a deep, narrow saucepan if possible. Ideally the asparagus should stand up in the pan with the tips just peeping out of the top. If you have to improvise, tie the asparagus together in a large bundle – this helps it to stand upright in the pan.

3. Bring some water to the boil in a kettle and pour it into the pan containing the asparagus spears until it covers the stems but not the tips. Add some salt.

4. Boil until the stems are just tender – the length of time will vary depending on the thickness of the spears. To test, pierce with a small sharp knife.

5. Drain and serve immediately. If serving cold, refresh with cold running water.

Asparagus with Prosciutto & Parmesan

This dish is really simple to make. It can be prepared in advance and finished under the grill at the last minute. Make sure you have an ovenproof serving dish large enough to take the asparagus lying flat without piling it up too much.

Method

1. Prepare the asparagus as described on p29. Be careful not to overcook it at this stage, as it will cook further when grilled. Drain and cool under running water. Preheat the grill.

2. Wrap a slice of prosciutto around the centre of two or three asparagus spears at a time, and then lay them in an ovenproof serving dish. Continue in this way until all the asparagus has been wrapped.

3. Sprinkle with a generous amount of freshly grated Parmesan cheese. Place under the grill until the Parmesan has melted and turned golden brown. Serve immediately. Delicious with new potatoes.

Ingredients

Per person

approximately 200g fresh asparagus

4 - 5 slices of prosciutto or Parma ham

Parmesan cheese, freshly grated

PARMESAN CHEESE

Authentic Parmigiano Reggiano, with its hard, grainy texture has D.O.P. status (protected designation of origin). It is made in a limited area of Emilia Romagna in Italy, where it is produced under strict conditions. Only unpasteurised milk produced between 1st May and 11th November by cattle fed on grass can be used. When the cheeses are 12 months old they must pass an assessment by a master grader who taps each massive 38kg cheese with a hammer. Only if he is satisfied that there are no cracks in the cheese will it be branded with the official logo. The tastiest Parmesan cheeses are aged for 3 years.

Chicken wrapped with Parma Ham & Basil

This is a variation of a recipe cooked for me by my sister, which has become a family favourite. Although other types of prosciutto can be used, authentic Parma ham gives the dish a lovely flavour. From a practical point of view, a slice is usually just the right size to make the parcel of chicken secure.

Method

1. Slice each of the chicken breasts in half lengthways.

2. Lay a piece of chicken diagonally across the corner of a slice of Parma ham and place two of the basil leaves on top. Roll up the chicken in the ham, keeping the basil leaves inside. Repeat with the remaining pieces of chicken.

3. Place a large, heavy-based frying or sauteuse pan over a moderate to high heat. Add the knob of butter, then quickly place the chicken rolls in the bottom of the pan. You may need to cook the chicken in batches if your pan is not large enough to take them all at once. Turn the chicken rolls several times so that they become browned all over and cooked through. This should take about 15 minutes.

4. Remove the chicken from the pan and keep warm in a serving dish. Return the pan to the heat and add the white wine. Allow it to bubble vigorously and reduce in quantity, stirring well so that it incorporates all the chicken juices.

5. When the wine has evaporated by about half, stir in the cream over the heat. Allow to bubble and thicken. Taste the sauce and season with a little salt and freshly ground black pepper.

6. Pour the hot cream sauce over the chicken pieces in the serving dish and sprinkle with chives. Serve with fresh seasonal vegetables and potatoes.

Ingredients

Serves 6

6 medium-sized raw chicken breasts

12 slices of Parma ham

24 fresh basil leaves

large knob of butter

100ml white wine

200ml double cream

salt & freshly ground black pepper

2 tablespoons fresh chives, chopped

Roast Leg of Spring Lamb

A field full of newborn lambs in early spring is a sign that we will soon be enjoying warmer weather and longer days.

In this recipe the lamb is studded with cloves of garlic and sprigs of rosemary – a classic combination of flavours. Don't worry if it is not tied with string as in our picture. Some butchers like to do this to help the meat keep its shape during roasting.

Method

1. Preheat the oven to 200°C (gas mark 6). Pat the surface of the meat dry with kitchen paper. With a small pointed knife, pierce the skin roughly every 2cm, making deep pockets in the meat.

2. Peel the cloves of garlic, and divide the rosemary into sprigs approximately 3cm in length. Push the garlic and rosemary alternately into the pockets you have made, tucking them in well. Rub the skin of the lamb with a little olive oil, then sprinkle with salt and freshly ground black pepper.

3. Lay the lamb in a roasting tin, preferably on a rack, and place in the preheated oven. Cook for 20 minutes per 500g, plus an extra 20 minutes. If you like your lamb quite pink, reduce the cooking time to 15 minutes per 500g, plus 15 minutes.

4. When the lamb is roasted to your taste remove it from the oven and leave to rest for 15 - 20 minutes before serving. If tied with string, remove before carving. Collect the meat juices in a jug and skim off any fat before reheating and pouring onto the tender sliced meat. Serve with fresh seasonal vegetables, Potato & Celeriac Dauphinoise (see recipe p192), or Puy Lentils with Rosemary & Chilli (see recipe p189).

Ingredients

Serves 8 - 10

- 1 leg of spring lamb, approximately 1.5 - 2kg in weight
- 1 garlic bulb, divided into cloves
- large bunch of fresh rosemary
- olive oil
- salt & freshly ground black pepper

ROSEMARY

Rosemary is one of the most versatile herbs in the kitchen. It has a distinctive pungent aroma which can be used to flavour both savoury and sweet dishes. Although it goes particularly well with roasted meats and stews, a small amount will enhance creamy desserts or poached fruit. Rosemary also aids digestion.

Veal Bocconcini

Literally translated, this means 'little mouthfuls of veal'. This recipe comes from Switzerland, where, if you walk as we do in the Alps in the summer, you will come across herds of cows with their calves grazing the high pastures. The Alpine meadows are carpeted with herbs and flowers which help to produce rich, nutty milk, cream and cheese and give the veal its distinctive flavour. This recipe allows for two bocconcini per person.

Method

1. Cut the veal into 12 equal slices. Place each slice between two pieces of cling film. Bat them out with a rolling pin until they are two to three millimetres thick. Cut the Gruyère cheese into 12 equal-sized pieces – these will form the centre of the stuffing for the veal rolls.

2. Spread the slices of veal out on the work surface. Lay a piece of Parma ham on each slice, followed by a piece of Gruyère. Roll up tightly and fasten securely with a cocktail stick or a piece of string. Season with salt and freshly ground black pepper.

3. Add the knob of butter to a large, heavy-based frying pan and brown the veal rolls, turning them carefully so that they colour on all sides.

4. Add the wine to the pan and cook for a further 10 minutes until the veal is tender and the sauce reduced to a coating consistency. Check for seasoning.

5. Remove the cocktail sticks or string, transfer the rolls of veal to a warm serving dish and ladle the sauce over the top. Serve immediately, sprinkled with fresh herbs. Delicious with Rösti (see recipe p155).

Ingredients

Serves 6

- **approximately 600g veal topside**
- **12 slices of Parma ham or prosciutto**
- **250g Gruyère cheese**
- **salt & freshly ground black pepper**
- **large knob of butter**
- **300ml dry white wine**
- **2 tablespoons fresh herbs such as parsley or chives, chopped**

Rhubarb Streusel Crumble

Tender pink shoots of rhubarb are one of the first things to emerge in our kitchen garden in spring. In this recipe almonds and hazelnuts are added to the traditional crumble topping giving it a tasty crunchy texture.

Method

1. Preheat the oven to 200°C (gas mark 6). Place the rhubarb and ginger in a heavy-based saucepan together with the sugar and orange juice. Simmer over a low heat for 10 - 15 minutes, until the rhubarb is tender. At this stage check whether you need to add more sugar, bearing in mind that the crumble topping is quite sweet. Tip into an ovenproof dish and allow to cool while you make the topping.

2. Put the flour, butter and caster sugar into a large mixing bowl. Rub the butter into the flour and sugar until the mixture resembles fine breadcrumbs. Stir in the ground and chopped almonds and the chopped hazelnuts. Mix well.

3. Spoon the streusel topping onto the rhubarb, spreading it evenly. Place in the preheated oven for approximately 20 minutes, until the top is golden. Serve with pouring cream or crème fraîche.

Ingredients

Serves 8

- 1kg rhubarb stalks, sliced into small chunks
- 50g fresh ginger, peeled and finely chopped
- approximately 100g caster sugar, depending on the sweetness of the rhubarb
- 100ml fresh orange juice

For the streusel topping

- 300g plain white flour
- 200g butter
- 100g caster sugar
- 80g ground almonds
- 80g chopped almonds
- 160g chopped hazelnuts

RHUBARB

Technically a vegetable, rhubarb is at its best in early spring. We grow 'Raspberry Red' which is deep red in colour and naturally quite sweet.

Chocolate Crème Brûlée

This rather indulgent variation of crème brûlée is my son's favourite dessert. The cream is enriched with plain dark chocolate, then finished in the traditional way with a crisp layer of caramelised sugar.

The key to success lies in the quality of the ingredients. The chocolate should have a cocoa-solid content of over 60%, and the cream should be double cream with a fat content of at least 40%. For a thin, crisp layer of caramelised sugar, use a cook's blowtorch. This will give the most professional result as it does not overheat the cream underneath. If you don't possess one, increase the depth of the sugar sprinkled on the top and place under a grill on its highest setting.

Start this dish a day before you wish to serve it. You could use the leftover egg whites to make a Pavlova (see recipe p101). Egg whites also keep well in the freezer for a couple of months.

Method

1. Preheat the oven to 160°C (gas mark 2½). Put the cream and chocolate pieces together in a medium-sized heavy-based saucepan and place over a low heat. Stir well until all the chocolate has melted. Now bring the mixture to just below boiling point and immediately remove from the heat. Allow to cool slightly.

2. In a large mixing bowl, lightly beat the egg yolks with a whisk. Gradually pour the chocolate and cream mixture into the yolks, whisking continuously until completely incorporated. Pass through a large sieve to remove any lumps.

3. Ladle the chocolate cream into one large or several individual dishes. Place them in a large roasting tin, then pour in sufficient boiling water to come halfway up the sides of the dishes. Bake in the preheated oven for approximately 10 - 15 minutes, until a thin skin forms on the top (a large dish will take longer). Remove from the oven, allow to cool and refrigerate overnight.

Ingredients

Makes approximately
8 individual or 1 large brûlée

175g best-quality plain dark chocolate, grated or chopped into small pieces

500ml double cream

4 egg yolks

caster sugar to caramelise the top

41

Chocolate Crème Brûlée

4. A couple of hours before you wish to serve the brûlées, make the caramelised sugar topping. Do not refrigerate afterwards – the moisture in the fridge will dissolve the caramel. If using a grill, turn it to its highest setting. Stand the dishes on a large sheet of greaseproof paper, then sprinkle the tops of the brûlées evenly with caster sugar. Collect the excess on the paper for re-use and wipe the rims of the dishes. To help dissolve the sugar, lightly mist the surface of the sugar with a little water, using a plant sprayer. Either melt the sugar using a cook's blowtorch, or grill the brûlées as close as possible to the heat until the sugar melts and caramelises. Allow to cool completely before serving.

COCOA

Columbus is credited with bringing cocoa from South America to Europe, probably on his fourth voyage in 1502. The Aztecs roasted and ground the seeds of the cocoa pod and made them into a drink which was said to have aphrodisiac properties. For several centuries Europeans consumed chocolate almost exclusively as a beverage until a technique was developed to dry and grind the beans, then heat them to melt the cocoa butter and form a paste. This was then allowed to solidify into lozenges, and chocolate as we know it was invented. These cocoa pods were grown by my father-in-law in his glasshouse in Harrogate.

Pancakes

Since the Middle Ages Shrove Tuesday has been a day of feasting and penitence. 'Shriving' is the name given to the ritual confession and absolution which traditionally took place on the day before Ash Wednesday when the Lenten fast began. During this period of 40 days and nights, devout Christians would deny themselves rich food such as eggs, milk and fat. Pancakes became associated with Shrove Tuesday as they were the perfect way to use up all these ingredients.

Pancakes can be refrigerated for several days or kept in the freezer, separated with pieces of greaseproof paper. To reheat return them briefly to the frying pan.

Method

1. Sift the flour and salt into a large mixing bowl. Make a well in the centre and pour in the egg mixture. With a hand whisk, begin to beat the eggs whilst starting to draw in the flour. Gradually add the milk, continuing to whisk until you have a batter the consistency of thin cream. Add two tablespoons of the melted butter and whisk again until completely smooth. Transfer the mixture to a large jug, cover and refrigerate for at least 30 minutes. This allows the starch in the flour to develop, which will make the pancakes light.

2. Place a medium-sized frying pan over a high heat, then quickly brush with a little of the melted butter. Immediately, pour in just enough batter to cover the base of the pan, tilting it and turning it to ensure the bottom of the pan is evenly coated. After about 30 seconds, lift the edge of the pancake with a palette knife to check if it is cooked. When it is golden-brown flip the pancake over to cook the other side. Remove from the pan and keep warm.

3. Continue in this way until all the batter has been used up. The pancakes should be very thin – if the first one is too thick, you may need to add a little more milk to the batter.

Ingredients

Makes approximately 8

110g plain white flour

pinch of salt

1 egg and 1 egg yolk, beaten

290ml semi-skimmed milk

50g butter, melted

To serve

caster sugar

freshly squeezed lemon or orange juice

lemon wedges or orange slices

Pancakes

4. Stack the cooked pancakes on top of each other, separated with pieces of greaseproof paper, cover and keep in a warm oven until you are ready to serve them.

5. To serve, sprinkle each pancake with caster sugar and freshly squeezed lemon or orange juice. Fold into quarters, arrange on a plate and sprinkle with a little more sugar and juice. Garnish with a lemon wedge or a slice of orange.

SAVOURY PANCAKES

Pancakes can also be served with a savoury filling such as Haddock & Prawn in Wine & Cream Sauce (see recipe p137), or Mushrooms in Wine & Cream (see recipe p129).

Caramelised Lemon Tart

Lemon tart is a simple, elegant dessert. Caramelising the top is optional – you will need a cook's blowtorch to do the job.

Double cream is used in the filling (rather than whipping or single) to give it a good dense texture. It is worth making your own sweet pastry, but if you are short of time, you could use shop-bought.

Method

1. First make the pastry as described on p232. Remove from the fridge and allow to almost reach room temperature. Lightly dust the work surface and rolling pin with flour and begin to roll out the pastry firmly but lightly. Keep turning it and dusting the work surface to ensure it doesn't stick. The pastry needs to be larger than your flan dish and approximately 3mm thick. Roll the pastry around the rolling pin and lift it over the flan dish. Gently coax it down the sides, making sure you don't stretch it. Trim off the excess with a sharp knife. Place the lined flan dish in the fridge and leave to rest for at least 20 minutes. Preheat the oven to 180°C (gas mark 4).

2. When the pastry has rested, take a piece of baking parchment a little larger than the flan dish, screw it into a ball, then flatten it out over the top of the pastry. Cover the surface with ceramic baking beans or rice. Bake in the oven for 10 minutes, then remove the paper and beans and return the dish to the oven for a further 5 - 10 minutes, until the pastry is set and slightly coloured. Turn the oven down to 150°C (gas mark 2).

3. Meanwhile, make the filling. Whisk the eggs with the sugar and the lemon zest, stir in the lemon juice and the double cream, trying not to make the mixture too frothy.

Ingredients

For a 28cm fluted flan dish
Serves 8 - 10

500g sweet pastry
(recipe p232)

8 medium eggs

350g caster sugar

4 unwaxed lemons: finely grated zest of 2 and juice of all 4

215g double cream

caster sugar to caramelise the top

Caramelised Lemon Tart

4. Slide out the oven shelf halfway, ensuring it is still secure and level. Put the pastry-lined flan dish onto a baking tray, then place on the shelf and pour the filling carefully into the warm pastry case. This avoids having to carry the full tart to the oven, risking spilling the mixture over the sides of the pastry which will make it stick. Bake for 45 - 50 minutes, or until the filling is just set – it should still wobble slightly when taken out of the oven. Allow to cool at room temperature.

5. To caramelise the top, sprinkle the whole surface of the tart with a layer of caster sugar, thick enough so you cannot see the colour of the filling. To help dissolve the sugar, lightly mist the surface with a little water, using a plant sprayer. With a cook's blowtorch, gradually melt the sugar until it is brown and brittle, taking care not to scorch the pastry at the edges. Once caramelised, do not put the tart back in the fridge – moisture will be drawn into the sugar, dissolving it. Serve with cream or crème fraîche.

LEMONS

Lemons are probably the most versatile and useful fruit in the kitchen. The zest and juice give freshness and flavour to endless dishes, dressings, sauces and desserts. Use organic unwaxed fruit if possible and choose fruit with firm, glossy yellow skin.

Hot Cross Buns

Traditionally eaten on Good Friday, hot cross buns have both heathen and Christian origins. It is said that in pagan times the buns were associated with ancient rituals surrounding the spring equinox – the cross representing the four quarters of the moon in perfect equilibrium. Subsequently, the Christian Church adopted the buns, reinterpreting the cross as a symbol of the Crucifixion. Although Queen Elizabeth I passed a law limiting the consumption of hot cross buns to proper religious festivals, nowadays they are available all year round. I think she had the right idea – things don't taste as special when you can eat them every day.

Method

For the crossing paste

This must be made a couple of hours before it is required to allow it to relax before piping.

1. Sieve the flour, salt and baking powder together into a small mixing bowl, then add the vegetable oil. Mix together until a crumb-like texture has formed.

2. Gradually add the water whilst beating with a wooden spoon until a smooth paste has formed. Beware, if you add the water too quickly it may become lumpy.

3. Once all the water has been incorporated, beat for a couple of minutes – this will develop the gluten in the mixture and give it elasticity. Leave the paste in the bowl and cover it with cling film to prevent skinning. Place in the fridge to relax.

For the hot cross buns and sugar-syrup glaze

1. Place the flour, sugar, salt and spice in a large mixing bowl. Add the butter or vegetable shortening. Rub the fat into the flour with your fingertips until the mixture resembles fine breadcrumbs and all the ingredients are evenly distributed.

Ingredients

Makes 12

For the crossing paste

180g strong white flour

pinch of salt

pinch of baking powder

50ml vegetable oil

120ml water

For the buns

400g strong white flour

60g caster sugar

1 level teaspoon salt

2 heaped teaspoons mixed spice

45g butter or vegetable shortening, cut into small pieces

50g fresh yeast (or 25g dried yeast)

130ml tepid water

70ml milk

100g currants

115g sultanas

50g chopped mixed peel

For the sugar-syrup glaze

200g caster sugar

200ml water

Hot Cross Buns

2. In a small bowl dissolve the yeast with the tepid water. Make a well in the centre of the flour mixture, then add the dissolved yeast and the milk. Gradually draw the flour away from the sides of the bowl into the centre to combine with the liquid, forming a dough.

3. Remove the dough from the bowl and knead for 10 – 12 minutes on a lightly floured surface until it is smooth and elastic.

4. Spread the dough out on the work surface and pile all of the dried fruit in the centre. Fold the outside edges around the fruit and continue to knead gently until the fruit is evenly distributed. At first it will be difficult to keep the fruit inside the dough, but perseverance will pay off. Leave to rest on the work surface for 5 minutes, covered with a clean tea towel.

5. Divide the dough into 12 equal portions with a metal scraper or a sharp knife (about 80g each) and shape into round balls. Line two baking sheets with baking parchment. Carefully place the buns on the baking sheets, leaving enough space between them to allow for rising. Cover with a clean, damp tea towel and leave to prove in a warm place until the buns have doubled in size and spring back slowly when pressed – this will take between 1 and 2 hours.

6. While the buns are proving preheat the oven to 200°C (gas mark 6) and prepare the sugar-syrup glaze. Combine the sugar and water in a small saucepan and bring to the boil. Keep the mixture boiling continuously until it becomes syrupy. Pour into a jug and allow to cool.

7. Once the buns have doubled in size, the crosses need to be added. Spoon the crossing paste into a piping bag and cut a small hole in the end. With a steady hand, pipe a cross on the top of each bun. Bake the buns in the preheated oven for 10 – 12 minutes until they are a rich golden brown.

8. Remove from the oven and immediately brush the tops of the buns with the sugar-syrup glaze. Transfer onto a cooling rack. Serve warm with butter.

Simnel Cake

Simnel cakes as we know them have been made since medieval times. It is believed that the word simnel has developed from the Latin word 'similia', meaning fine wheaten flour. Simnel cakes were traditionally baked during the Lenten fast and became connected with Mothering Sunday in the 17th century when girls in domestic service returned home to visit their mothers with gifts of Simnel cakes and freshly picked spring flowers.

These days, Simnel cakes are associated with the religious festival of Easter. Traditionally they are decorated with eleven balls of marzipan, representing the eleven faithful disciples of Christ.

This is my favourite fruit cake recipe. The layer of marzipan through the centre of the cake makes it wonderfully moist and it is really worth making your own (see recipe p235) – the texture and flavour is so superior to shop-bought. Bake the cake several weeks in advance to allow it to mature, and decorate one or two days before you want to serve it.

One of my favourite heirlooms is a magnificent handmade crocheted linen Stilton frill which I use to decorate the outside of our Simnel cake.

Method

1. Preheat the oven to 145°C (gas mark 1½). Take roughly one third of the home-made marzipan, then wrap the rest in foil and store in the fridge until needed to decorate the cake. Sprinkle the work surface with icing sugar and roll out the marzipan until it is slightly larger than the base of a 20cm diameter x 8cm deep loose-bottomed cake tin. Using the base of the cake tin as a guide, cut out a circle of marzipan. Set aside.

2. Line the sides and bottom of the cake tin with baking parchment.

Ingredients

Makes a 20cm diameter cake

1kg home-made marzipan (recipe p235)

260g butter

260g caster sugar

4 large eggs

350g plain white flour

pinch of salt

¾ teaspoon freshly grated nutmeg

¾ teaspoon ground cinnamon

350g raisins } soaked in 50ml sherry for
175g sultanas } several hours

150g whole mixed peel (lemon, orange and citron), finely chopped

200g naturally coloured glacé cherries

For the decoration

remaining marzipan

2 teaspoons apricot jam

2 teaspoons water

1 egg, beaten

Simnel Cake

3. Beat together the butter and the sugar in a large mixing bowl until pale and creamy. Add the eggs, one by one, mixing in well.

4. Blend together the flour, salt and spices and add gradually to the mixture. Add the sherry, raisins and sultanas, followed by the peel. Gently stir in the cherries so that they remain whole.

5. Spoon half the mixture into the cake tin and flatten. Place the circle of marzipan on top and then add the rest of the cake mixture to fill the cake tin.

6. Bake in the preheated oven for approximately 2½ hours. The cake will be ready when it is golden brown on top and firm to the touch. Pierce the centre with a thin skewer – it should come out clean.

7. When cool enough to handle, remove from the cake tin and leave to cool on a cooling rack. To store, wrap in tin foil and place in an airtight container in a cool place.

To decorate

1. Divide the remaining marzipan into two halves. With one half make eleven round balls. Roll out the second half until you have a circle of marzipan large enough to cover the top of the cake. Using the base of the cake tin as a guide, cut out a circle of marzipan as before. Set aside.

2. Combine the apricot jam and water in a small pan and heat gently until the mixture becomes syrupy. Allow to cool slightly then brush over the surface of the cake.

3. Preheat the grill. Carefully lift the marzipan onto the top of the cake and press gently with the rolling pin to flatten the surface.

4. Create your own artistic patterns on the marzipan – I use a broad-bladed knife to make a criss-cross pattern.

5. Once you are happy with your design, brush the surface sparingly with the beaten egg and immediately place the cake under the grill. Watch carefully as the marzipan colours very quickly. When it has turned a pale, golden brown remove it immediately.

6. Now place your marzipan balls evenly around the edge of the cake, pressing them onto the toasted marzipan. Brush the tops of the balls with beaten egg and place under the grill again. Remove when both cake and balls are a deep golden brown.

7. When cool, cover the sides of the cake as desired.

Simnel Cake

Swiss Chocolate & Hazelnut Cake

The joy of this delicious, moist gluten-free cake is that it is really simple to make. Use the best-quality chocolate you can find – the higher the cocoa solids the better. Although very rich, it is not too sweet and will improve with keeping, so is best made a couple of days in advance. It also keeps for several weeks in the freezer. For a nut-free cake, replace the ground hazelnuts with plain white flour.

Method

1. Line the base and sides of a 23cm round cake tin (preferably springform or loose-bottomed) with baking parchment, using a little melted butter under the parchment to help it stay in place. Preheat your oven to 180°C (gas mark 4).

2. Place the chocolate and water together in a fairly large, heavy-based saucepan and melt very gently over a low heat, stirring until smooth and amalgamated. Remove from the heat and whisk in the butter and egg yolks. Stir in the hazelnuts and Kirsch. Set aside to cool.

3. Beat the egg whites together with the salt in a large clean mixing bowl until they are fairly stiff. Gradually add the sugar whilst still beating until the mixture is thick and glossy. Gently fold into the chocolate mixture, one spoonful at a time taking care not to knock the air out of the egg whites.

4. Pour into the prepared cake tin and place in the preheated oven for approximately 40 - 45 minutes, until risen and firm to the touch. To check that it is ready, pierce the centre with a thin skewer – it should come out clean. Allow to stand for a few minutes in the cake tin, then remove and leave to cool on a cooling rack.

5. To decorate, dust with either icing sugar or cocoa powder.

Ingredients

Makes a 23cm diameter cake
Serves 10 - 12

- 150g best-quality plain dark chocolate, broken into pieces
- 2 tablespoons water
- 125g butter, cut into small pieces
- 6 large eggs, separated
- 180g ground hazelnuts
- 1 tablespoon Kirsch
- pinch of salt
- 75g caster sugar
- icing sugar or cocoa powder for dusting

HAZELNUTS

These delicious nuts, known since the time of the Ancient Greeks, have a special affinity with chocolate. The Romans associated hazelnut wood with fertility, others believed that eating the nuts could help conquer the common cold. The English variety, found in autumn hedgerows, is known as a 'Filbert'.

Elderflower Cordial

Home-made elderflower cordial is absolutely delicious and very simple to make. The undiluted syrup can also be drizzled over sliced strawberries instead of sugar. For best results pick the elderflowers when they have just opened and are full of pollen.

Citric acid can be hard to find – try your local chemist.

This cordial keeps well in the freezer, so even in the depths of winter you can enjoy a taste of spring.

Method

1. Place the elderflowers in a large bowl.

2. Put the sugar and water into a large, heavy-based pan and place over a low heat. Stir until the sugar is dissolved and then bring the mixture to the boil. Remove from the heat and add the citric acid.

3. Allow the mixture to cool and pour over the elderflowers.

4. Remove the zest from the outside of the lemons with a grater, then roughly slice the lemons. Add both to the mixture and stir gently. Cover and leave in a cool place for 24 hours.

5. Strain through a colander lined with muslin and store in bottles in the fridge. If freezing, use plastic bottles. To serve, dilute to taste with either sparkling or still water.

Ingredients

Makes approximately 2 litres of syrup, before diluting

20 large elderflower heads, without leaves

1.8kg granulated sugar

1 litre water

75g citric acid

2 lemons

Bircher Muesli

Although Bircher Muesli is most commonly eaten at breakfast, it is a wonderfully nourishing dish which can be enjoyed at any time of the day. Oats, the major ingredient, release their energy slowly into the body, keeping blood sugar levels steady and hunger pangs at bay.

This dish was invented by Dr. Bircher-Benner, a Swiss pioneer of nutrition who was working in Zürich in the late 1890s. Then, as now, there was a huge amount of interest in the connection between good health and diet – it is said that the learned doctor cured himself of jaundice by restricting his diet to raw apples. His muesli was designed to contain all the necessary nutrients, vitamins and minerals required to sustain the human body, in one dish.

The base mix needs to be made a few hours before it is required, and can be kept refrigerated for several days. If you are avoiding dairy products, substitute extra juice in place of the milk. Feel free to add whatever else takes your fancy – honey, yoghurt or seasonal fruit.

This is an original Swiss recipe, given to me by my father-in-law, Victor. Once you have tasted it, I can guarantee you will never want to eat dried packet muesli again.

Method

1. Mix all the ingredients together in a large bowl.

2. Leave to stand for a few hours. The texture should be similar to porridge. If it is a little too thick, add more milk or juice.

3. Before serving, coarsely grate two eating apples, leaving the skins on, and add to the mix.

4. Spoon into bowls, adding whatever fresh seasonal fruit you have to hand.

Ingredients

Serves approximately 5 - 6

150g oatflakes

50g sultanas

50g chopped hazelnuts

200ml milk

200ml fresh orange juice

juice of ½ a lemon

two apples, for serving

APPLES

We grow two varieties of apple in our garden, 'Discovery' and 'Cox's Orange Pippin'. 'Discovery', pictured above, are the first to ripen and have vivid red skins with rose-tinted flesh. Red apples contain twice as many of the disease-fighting antioxidants – polyphenols – as green apples; with the skins containing five times as many as the flesh. All apples contain pectin – a soluble fibre which helps lower cholesterol.

Summer

Recipes

Garden Vegetable Soup

The ingredients for this soup can be varied to make use of whatever you have available in the garden, or whatever is cheap and in plentiful supply in the shops. For a vegetarian version, leave out the bacon.

Method

1. Sweat the onion in the oil in a large, heavy-based saucepan. Add the garlic and bacon. Allow to soften but not colour.

2. Add the carrots, celery, potatoes and tomatoes and cover with the stock. Bring the soup to the boil and simmer gently until the vegetables are tender but not over cooked – approximately 10 – 15 minutes.

3. Add the beans or peas and simmer for another 2 – 3 minutes.

4. Finally, add the courgettes and bring back to the boil.

5. Season with salt and freshly ground black pepper to taste.

6. To serve, sprinkle with fresh herbs of your choice.

Ingredients

Serves 4 - 6

1 tablespoon oil

1 large onion, finely chopped

2 garlic cloves, crushed

2 rashers of bacon, finely chopped

2 medium carrots, finely diced

1 stick of celery, finely sliced

2 medium potatoes, peeled and finely diced

3 large tomatoes, peeled and chopped

1 litre vegetable stock (recipe p237), or vegetable bouillon

handful of broad beans or fresh garden peas

2 small courgettes, finely diced

salt & freshly ground black pepper

fresh herbs, chopped

Focaccia al Rosmarino

Focaccia is an Italian flat bread from Liguria, the beautiful coastal region between the French Riviera and Tuscany. A simple, rustic recipe in Roman times, it has become a modern delicacy, often studded with olives, onions or cheese, but always drizzled with local olive oil and sprinkled with coarse salt.

Method

1. First make the starter. Mix the yeast and the tepid water together in a jug. Place the flour in a small bowl and make a well in the centre. Add the yeast and water mixture and whisk together using a fork, until smooth. Cover with cling film and set aside for at least 30 minutes.

2. Next prepare the dough. Place the flour, salt and rosemary together in a large mixing bowl. Make a well and add the olive oil followed by the prepared starter. Gradually draw the flour away from the sides of the bowl into the centre to combine with the oil and starter, forming a dough.

3. Remove the dough from the bowl and knead for 10 minutes on a lightly floured surface until it is smooth and elastic.

4. Place the dough back in the bowl, cover with cling film and allow to rest in a warm place for 1 - 2 hours, until it is doubled in size.

5. Remove the dough from the bowl and knead again for 1 - 2 minutes; this redistributes the yeast and evens out the texture of the bread by removing any air bubbles which have formed during rising.

6. Mould into a round ball, cover with a clean tea towel and leave to rest on the work surface for a few minutes until the dough feels relaxed. Line a baking tray with baking parchment.

Ingredients

Makes 1 focaccia

For the starter

10g fresh yeast
  (or 5g dried yeast)

150ml tepid water

50g strong white flour

For the dough

200g strong white flour

¾ teaspoon salt

2 tablespoons fresh
  rosemary, finely chopped

1 tablespoon extra virgin
  olive oil

For the topping

extra virgin olive oil

coarse sea salt

sprig of fresh rosemary

olives, optional

Focaccia al Rosmarino

7. Using a rolling pin, roll out the dough, shaping it into a circle about 16cm in diameter. Transfer to the lined baking tray and leave in a warm, humid place to prove for roughly 1 hour. Preheat the oven to 200°C (gas mark 6).

8. When risen and proved, gently make dimples in the top of the focaccia with your fingers. Drizzle the top with a generous quantity of olive oil and sprinkle with the coarse sea salt. Decorate with fresh rosemary. At this stage, you could press olives into the top.

9. Place in the preheated oven and bake until golden – approximately 15 minutes.

10. Remove from the oven and leave to cool on a cooling rack.

Bruschette

These slices of toasted bread, brushed with olive oil, rubbed with garlic and covered with various delicious toppings, make an ideal al fresco first course.

Method

1. Preheat the oven to 200°C (gas mark 6). Cut the bread into slices roughly 2cm thick. Brush one side with the olive oil and rub with the cut side of the garlic clove.

2. Lay the slices of bread on a large baking sheet, oiled side up, and place in the preheated oven until slightly browned – approximately 5 minutes.

3. Cover with your favourite toppings and serve immediately.

Cheese & Herb Pâté

This is a simple and tasty pâté, perfect for spreading on a slice of crusty bread or filling Parmesan Choux Puffs (see recipe p72). It is best made in summer when herbs are at their freshest, and keeps well in the fridge for up to a week.

Method

1. Mix the cream cheese, garlic, salt, parsley, chives and chervil together in a bowl, making sure the herbs are evenly distributed.

2. Slowly melt the butter in a small saucepan – do not allow it to burn. Cool to the point where it can still be poured, but has not yet solidified.

3. Stir the liquid butter gently into the cream cheese mixture, then place in the fridge to set.

Ingredients

a loaf of bread – ciabatta or similar

extra virgin olive oil

1 garlic clove, cut in half

toppings of your choice, for example – chopped tomatoes with basil, Parma ham and rocket, roasted peppers, mozzarella cheese, Parmesan shavings, sun-dried tomatoes, grilled aubergines, Cheese & Herb Pâté (recipe below)

Ingredients

Makes approximately 300g

225g cream cheese

1 large garlic clove, crushed

pinch of salt

1 tablespoon each of fresh parsley, chives and chervil, finely chopped

75g butter

Ingredients

Makes approximately 40

100g butter, cut into small
    pieces

½ teaspoon salt

250ml water

150g plain flour

4 large eggs

60g Parmesan cheese,
    freshly grated

Parmesan Choux Puffs

Choux pastry is really quite a simple thing to make. It can
be filled with a variety of delicious fillings, both savoury
and sweet. The choux in this recipe is flavoured with grated
Parmesan cheese and the puffs can be eaten on their own
or filled with savoury pâté. Store in an airtight container for
2 - 3 days, or keep in the freezer for several weeks.

To make sweet choux puffs, omit the Parmesan cheese. Fill
with crème pâtissière (see recipe p244) and serve with
chocolate sauce (see recipe p243) to make delicious profiteroles.

Method

1. Preheat the oven to 200°C (gas mark 6). Line a large
   baking sheet with baking parchment.

2. Place the butter in a medium, heavy-based saucepan with
   the salt and water. Heat until it has melted and the water
   has come to the boil. Remove immediately from the heat –
   prolonged boiling evaporates the water and will change the
   proportions of the dough. As soon as the pan is removed,
   add all the flour in one go whilst beating with a hand
   whisk. After about a minute the mixture should become
   smooth and pull away from the pan to form a stiff ball.

3. Beat the eggs into the mixture one by one, making sure
   each one is thoroughly incorporated before adding the next.
   The mixture should become shiny and just soft enough to
   fall off a spoon. Beat in the Parmesan cheese.

4. Using a piping bag, pipe small mounds of mixture roughly
   3cm in diameter onto the lined baking sheet, leaving
   plenty of room for the puffs to expand during baking.

5. Bake for 15 - 18 minutes, until risen and brown. Don't be
   tempted to remove from the oven too soon or they will
   collapse – the dough needs to be thoroughly dry and crisp.
   Transfer to a cooling rack. To serve, fill with Cheese & Herb
   Pâté (see recipe p69) or Mushroom Pâté (see recipe p125).

Coronation Chicken

Coronation chicken was served at the banquet following Queen Elizabeth II's coronation in 1953. It was created by Constance Spry and Rosemary Hume, whose wonderful cookery book I still use regularly.

This version is slightly lighter than the original and goes very well with the simple Saffron Rice Salad (see recipe overleaf). It is also delicious with Couscous Salad (see recipe p93).

Method

1. First prepare the chicken. Preheat the oven to 180°C (gas mark 4), lay the chicken breasts on a baking tray, season with salt and freshly ground black pepper, dot with the butter and cover with baking foil. Place in the preheated oven for 20 – 30 minutes (depending on the thickness of the breasts) until the chicken is cooked through but not browned. Set aside to cool.

2. Next prepare the curry dressing. Heat 1 tablespoon of the oil in a small, heavy-based saucepan and add the onion. Sauté over a moderate heat until soft and translucent but not browned. Add the curry powder and cook gently for a further 2 minutes, stirring well with a metal spoon. Next add the tomato purée, water and vinegar and leave to simmer until reduced by half. Remove from the heat, stir in the apricot jam and leave to cool.

3. Transfer the mixture to a food processor or container suitable for use with a hand blender. Process until smooth. Add the lemon juice and cottage cheese and continue blending until smooth once again. Whilst still blending gradually add the remainder of the oil. The dressing should be thick and creamy in texture. Check for seasoning.

4. Tear the chicken breasts into pieces and place in a large bowl. Add the curry dressing and stir gently to coat the chicken evenly. Transfer to a serving dish and sprinkle with paprika. Garnish with coriander or flat-leaved parsley.

Ingredients

Serves 6 – 8

1kg raw chicken breasts

salt & freshly ground black pepper

large knob of butter

1 small onion, finely chopped

1 tablespoon curry powder

1 tablespoon tomato purée

3 tablespoons water

4 tablespoons red wine vinegar

2 teaspoons apricot jam

2 tablespoons freshly squeezed lemon juice

250g cottage cheese

90ml sunflower oil

paprika and fresh coriander or flat-leaved parsley for decoration

Ingredients

Serves 6 - 8

several pinches of saffron
strands

½ teaspoon salt

600ml water

300g basmati rice

3 sticks of celery, thinly
sliced

1 tablespoon fresh coriander
or flat-leaved parsley,
chopped

For the dressing

2 tablespoons freshly
squeezed lemon juice

salt & freshly ground
black pepper

6 tablespoons sunflower oil

FLAT-LEAVED PARSLEY

Sometimes called Italian parsley, this
herb is not only decorative but full
of goodness. It contains high levels of
vitamins A and C, potassium, calcium,
phosphorus, magnesium and iron.

Saffron Rice Salad

Method

1. Put the saffron, salt and water into a large, heavy-based
saucepan. Bring to the boil and simmer for a couple of
minutes. Add the rice, bring back to the boil, then cover
and simmer until the rice is tender and all the water is
absorbed – approximately 15 - 20 minutes. Leave to cool
for 10 minutes, then stir with a fork.

2. Stir the celery and herbs into the cooked saffron rice with
a fork. Transfer to a bowl.

3. To make the dressing, put the lemon juice, salt, and freshly
ground black pepper into a jug. Add the sunflower oil
whilst whisking so that the dressing thickens slightly.

4. Pour the dressing over the rice and toss gently with a fork
to combine. Transfer to a serving dish.

Slow-roasted Tomato & Mozzarella Salad

Roasting tomatoes slowly in the oven intensifies both their flavour and colour. They can be prepared in advance and keep well in the fridge for several days. Plum tomatoes are the most suitable for this dish: they are full of flavour but not too juicy. Fresh basil is essential and is easy to grow on a windowsill in summer. This salad makes a delicious starter or can be eaten as a main course with fresh crusty bread – adjust the quantities accordingly.

Method

1. Preheat the oven to 110°C (gas mark ½). Slice the tomatoes in half lengthways and place in a mixing bowl. Add the garlic, drizzle with a generous quantity of olive oil and sprinkle with salt and freshly ground black pepper. Add a few torn basil leaves and turn with a wooden spoon until all the ingredients are mixed together well.

2. Arrange on a baking tray, spreading the tomatoes out so that the cut side is uppermost and they are not piled on top of each other. Place in the preheated oven for approximately 2½ - 3 hours. Remove from the oven when they have shrunk in size and look slightly shrivelled.

3. When the tomatoes are completely cool, spread the salad leaves on the bottom of a flat serving dish. Arrange the tomatoes on top. Drain the mozzarella cheese, slice and arrange evenly between the tomatoes. Sprinkle the onion slices and torn basil leaves over the tomatoes and cheese.

4. To make the balsamic vinegar dressing, mix together the olive oil and balsamic vinegar, stirring well to amalgamate. Finally drizzle the dressing over the salad.

Ingredients

Serves 4 as a main course

- **16 medium plum tomatoes**
- **2 garlic cloves, crushed**
- **extra virgin olive oil**
- **salt & freshly ground black pepper**
- **handful of fresh basil leaves**
- **fresh garden salad leaves**
- **500g buffalo mozzarella cheese**
- **1 red onion, finely sliced**

For the dressing

- **6 tablespoons extra virgin olive oil**
- **2 tablespoons balsamic vinegar**

TOMATOES

Characterised by their elongated shape, 'San Marzano' plum tomatoes come from the Campania area of Italy where they have D.O.P. status. These were grown in our greenhouse.

Salade Niçoise

Salade Niçoise is one of the great salad classics. Translated literally, it means 'Nice-style salad', named after the city on the French Riviera where it originated. The ingredients vary from restaurant to restaurant; however most agree that the essentials for a good Salade Niçoise are ripe tomatoes, garlic, olives and anchovies with crisp lettuce, crunchy French beans and perfectly boiled eggs.

Method

1. Top and tail the beans and cook them in salted boiling water for 2 - 3 minutes. Refresh under cold running water – they should retain their bright green colour and still be slightly crisp.

2. Boil the eggs for 6 - 7 minutes, until they are only just set. Plunge them immediately into cold running water to stop them cooking further and prevent dark circles from forming around the yolks. When cool, peel and quarter them.

3. Place the tomatoes in a bowl and cover them with boiling water. After about half a minute, pour the water away and remove the skins. Cut into segments.

4. Carefully rinse the anchovies under running water, removing any bones that are visible.

5. Next make the dressing. Whisk the vinegar and mustard together with the garlic, salt and freshly ground black pepper. Drizzle in the oil whilst still whisking.

6. Cook the tuna briefly on both sides in a griddle pan – it is important it remains moist. Break into bite-sized pieces.

7. Place the washed lettuce leaves in a large shallow bowl, tearing them into smaller pieces if necessary. Arrange the tomatoes, French beans, tuna, eggs, anchovy fillets and olives on top of the leaves. Sprinkle with the fresh herbs. Finally, drizzle the dressing over the whole salad. Serve with fresh crusty bread.

Ingredients

Serves 4

100g French beans

4 eggs

4 ripe tomatoes (traditionally 'Marmande' are used)

8 anchovy fillets

400g fresh tuna

300g little gem lettuce leaves

handful of black olives

1 tablespoon fresh herbs such as parsley, chives and chervil, chopped

For the dressing

2 tablespoons white wine vinegar

½ teaspoon Dijon mustard

1 garlic clove, crushed

salt & freshly ground black pepper

6 tablespoons extra virgin olive oil

Ingredients

Makes approximately 500ml

175ml extra virgin olive oil
  (preferably Ligurian)

75g pine nuts

1 garlic clove, with centre
  removed

150g fresh, small, young
  basil leaves, (about 3 large
  shop-bought pots)

a couple of ice cubes

100g Parmesan cheese,
  freshly grated

salt

Corrado Corti, Chef de Cuisine of
the Splendido Hotel in Portofino

Fresh Pesto

Pesto is a speciality of Liguria, the coastal region between
the French Riviera and Tuscany. My Ligurian friends are
adamant that the area around Genoa is the only place
authentic pesto can be made. They use young basil leaves,
grown in Prà, a suburb of the city, where the temperature
in winter never falls below 7°C. Here, the free-draining
soil contains particular minerals which give the basil its
distinctive flavour and it is harvested when the delicate oils
in the leaves are at their most potent. As a result of all the
care and attention lavished on this most fragrant of herbs,
Genoese Basil (*Ocimum basilicum* – meaning 'regal scent') has
been awarded D.O.P. status (protected designation of origin).
So, I can understand why the Ligurians might think that we
should stick to our Yorkshire puddings. However, I believe
that it is possible to make a pretty good version of fresh pesto
in this country, provided a few simple rules are followed.
Recently, I was invited into the kitchens of the superb Hotel
Splendido in Portofino by Chef de Cuisine, Corrado Corti,
who shared his tips with me:-

- always use small, fresh basil leaves from a young plant,
  never use a packet of ready-picked leaves. Basil is quite
  an easy plant to grow on a sunny windowsill or in a
  warm greenhouse.

- only use the leaves of the plant – stalks will make the
  pesto bitter.

- keep all your ingredients as cool as possible – remove
  them from the fridge at the last minute. This recipe
  includes a few ice cubes which are essential to keep the
  pesto cool while it is being processed.

- keep the processing to a minimum. The word 'pesto'
  means pestle – pesto would traditionally have been made
  in a pestle and mortar. These days, most chefs use a food
  processor or hand blender which can encourage over
  blending and lead to oxidation and discolouration.

- if possible, use Ligurian olive oil – as it is produced in the same area as the basil, it adds to the authentic flavour.

- always remove the tiny centre from cloves of garlic, which will eventually sprout. If left, they will make the pesto bitter.

Fresh pesto will keep for several weeks in a sealed container in the fridge. Cover the surface with a thin layer of oil to prevent discolouration. I have also frozen pesto successfully, something I am sure no self-respecting Ligurian would do.

Traditionally, pesto is served with trofie pasta (see recipe overleaf), but it is also a delicious accompaniment for grilled fish or meat.

Method

1. Place approximately 50ml of the oil in a food processor together with the pine nuts and garlic clove. Blend for a few seconds until a paste has formed.

2. Add the remainder of the oil together with the basil leaves and a couple of ice cubes. Blend briefly until the basil has been amalgamated into the paste.

3. Finally, stir in the Parmesan cheese and season with salt to taste.

Trofie with Pesto

In Liguria, pesto is served with trofie – handmade small twisted pasta dumplings. To be completely authentic, green beans and potato are added to the trofie as it cooks. Both fresh and dried trofie is readily available these days, but you could use pasta of any shape or size.

Method

1. Bring a large, heavy-based pan of salted water to the boil. Add the trofie, potato and green beans. Bring back to the boil and simmer gently according to the instructions on the packet (for dried trofie roughly 8 minutes).

2. When the trofie is cooked, but still firm ('al dente' – literally 'with a bit of a bite'), drain well and transfer to a bowl. Spoon the pesto over the top, then toss carefully so that everything is well coated.

3. Serve immediately, with a generous sprinkling of freshly grated Parmesan cheese.

Ingredients

Per person

approximately 125g trofie

75g waxy potatoes, cut into small cubes

75g green beans, cut into lengths of about 4cm

approximately 2 tablespoons Pesto (recipe p80)

Parmesan cheese for serving, freshly grated

FRENCH BEANS

There are many types of French bean – we grow 'Aiguillono' – a dwarf variety. To prepare as a side dish, first bring a pan of salted water to the boil. Top, tail and wash the beans, then toss into the boiling water. Cook until just tender. Alternatively, braise them in onion, garlic and chopped tomatoes for roughly 20 minutes, to give them a provençale flavour.

Ingredients

Per person

a little sunflower oil

large knob of butter

½ tablespoon carrot, cut into very fine strips

½ tablespoon leek or shallot, cut into very fine strips

1 teaspoon fresh herbs such as dill, flat-leaved parsley and chives, chopped

salt & freshly ground black pepper

1 salmon fillet, approximately 150 – 170g in weight

1 teaspoon freshly squeezed lemon juice

1 tablespoon white wine

A papillote made from baking parchment

Salmon en Papillote

A 'papillote' is an envelope made from baking parchment or foil. A portion of meat or fish is placed inside, together with thin strips of vegetables, herbs, a little white wine, lemon juice and a dot of butter. The contents bake in their own juices, remaining moist and succulent. This is the perfect way to bake fish and chicken, both of which have a tendency to dry out. It is worth buying wild salmon – even organic farmed salmon is flabby and fatty.

Method

1. Cut out a circle of baking parchment or foil per person, approximately 30cm in diameter. Alternatively, make one circle or rectangle large enough to take all the portions of salmon. Brush with a little oil. Preheat the oven to 220°C (gas mark 7) and place a baking tray in it to warm up.

2. Melt half the butter in a frying pan, add the carrot and leek and allow to soften (but not brown) for several minutes. Add the herbs and season with salt and freshly ground black pepper. Set aside to cool.

3. Lay each salmon fillet onto the prepared parchment or foil. Season with a little more salt and pepper. Spread the prepared vegetables on the top, drizzle with the lemon juice and white wine and dot with the remaining butter. Fold the other half of the parchment or foil over the fish and seal the round edge by twisting and folding the two edges together. It should resemble a large Cornish pasty when finished.

4. Lay on the hot baking tray and place in the preheated oven for approximately 12 – 15 minutes. The fish should feel firm when pressed through the paper.

5. Serve hot with hollandaise sauce (see recipe p238), or alternatively allow to cool inside the envelope and serve with mayonnaise (see recipe p239). Delicious with Cucumber & Herb Salad (see recipe opposite).

Cucumber & Herb Salad

Home-grown cucumbers look, feel and taste completely different from the plastic-skinned, watery cucumbers found in our supermarkets. This is a simple salad, light and summery – ideal for serving with cold fish or meat.

Method

1. Peel the cucumber with a vegetable peeler, then cut in half lengthways. Scoop the seeds out of the centre all the way down the length of the cucumber, using a small teaspoon. Chop into slices approximately ½cm thick.

2. Place the grated zest and lemon juice in a bowl. Add the dill and chives, vinegar, crème fraîche, mustard and salt and pepper. Mix thoroughly.

3. Add the sliced cucumber, stirring gently until it is completely coated with the dressing.

Ingredients

Serves 4 – 6 as an accompaniment

- 1 cucumber (roughly 350g)

- grated zest and juice of ½ a lemon

- 1 tablespoon fresh dill, chopped

- 1 tablespoon fresh chives, chopped

- 1 tablespoon white wine vinegar

- 100ml crème fraîche

- 1 teaspoon Dijon mustard

- salt & freshly ground black pepper

CUCUMBER

Home-grown cucumbers have a crisp texture and sweet flavour which goes particularly well with fish and grilled meats. This variety is 'Cetriolo Sakamari', grown in our greenhouse at home.

Garden Potatoes

Potatoes straight from the soil have a flavour and texture all of their own. I always feel that summer has arrived when we sit down to eat the first small new potatoes from our garden. The seed potatoes are planted, as is the tradition, on Good Friday and the first earlies are usually ready by the end of June. We grow three varieties, giving us a successional crop which lasts until late autumn.

'Arran Pilot' – *first early*

These potatoes have firm, white flesh with a delicate flavour and waxy texture. They are best boiled in salted water until tender and served with a little melted butter and chopped parsley or chives.

'Charlotte' – *second early*

'Charlottes' follow on from the 'Arran Pilots'. They are oval in shape with a smooth skin. The flesh is creamy in colour and has a waxy texture, delicious in potato salads. If they are allowed to grow to a good size, they can be used in dishes such as Potato & Celeriac Dauphinoise (see recipe p192) or Rösti (see recipe p155).

'Pink Fir Apple' – *late main crop*

These are the last potatoes of the year. 'Pink Fir Apple' is a traditional variety which is over 100 years old. It has a distinctive knobbly shape with deep-pink skin. The flesh is creamy yellow in colour and firm and waxy in texture. Although they are fiddly to wash and prepare, it is worth the effort. Boil until tender and serve with melted better and chopped herbs. Delicious with Grilled Raclette (see recipe p185).

Globe Artichokes

This ancient vegetable, known since Greek and Roman times, is actually the unopened flower of an edible thistle. Artichoke leaves should be tightly closed – if there is any opening from the centre it is a sign that they are coming into flower and are past their best. Large parts of the plant are too tough to eat – only the fleshy base of the leaves and the tender heart at the centre are really succulent.

To prepare, remove the fibrous stalk and tear off any tough or discoloured outer leaves. Simmer for 20 - 25 minutes in a large pan of salted water with a little lemon juice added. When ready, the base of the vegetable will pierce easily with a skewer or small knife.

To eat, tear off the individual leaves from the outside of the artichoke, dip the fleshy end in hollandaise sauce (see recipe p238) or French dressing (see recipe p240), and scrape the flesh away with your teeth, discarding the remainder of the leaf. Work your way, leaf by leaf to the centre of the vegetable. When you have exposed the hairy 'choke' remove it with a teaspoon and enjoy the heart with a little more sauce.

Salad Leaves

We grow a large array of salad leaves and lettuces in our kitchen garden, giving us variety and colour all through summer, autumn and even into winter. Rocket leaves are the first to be ready – at the beginning of May if the weather is warm. We also grow wild rocket which has a finer, serrated leaf. Both have a peppery flavour which becomes stronger as the leaves grow larger.

Summer lettuce varieties include 'Red Oakleaf', 'Freckles' – with a pretty speckled leaf, 'Salad Bowl', 'Lollo Rosso' and 'Mixed Leaves'. In autumn we have red and green chicory and endive, followed by lamb's lettuce, which is tough enough to survive northern winters.

Lamb Brochettes

Eating outside is one of the great pleasures of an English summer – even better if the food can be grilled on a barbecue whilst you sip a cool aperitif. However, these delicious skewers of tender, boned, marinated lamb can be cooked just as easily indoors under a hot grill should the English weather turn inclement. To ensure the lamb is really tender, marinate it overnight. Delicious with Couscous Salad (see recipe overleaf), Courgettes Provençales (see recipe overleaf) and new potatoes.

Method

1. Cut the boned lamb into cubes approximately 2½cm in size. Place them in a large bowl with the onions, garlic and bay leaves. Season well. Pour the olive oil and dry martini over the lamb, stirring well to coat all of the meat. Leave overnight in the fridge.

2. Remove the pieces of lamb and onion from the marinade, reserving the liquid in a jug. This can be used to baste the skewers of meat whilst they grill.

3. Make up the brochettes, alternating pieces of meat with onion and vegetables. Place on the barbecue or under a hot grill, until the lamb is browned and the vegetables slightly charred.

Ingredients

Makes 6 brochettes

- 1 boned leg of lamb, roughly 1kg in weight
- 3 medium onions, quartered
- 2 garlic cloves, sliced
- 4 bay leaves
- 100ml extra virgin olive oil
- 50ml dry martini
- salt & freshly ground black pepper
- a selection of seasonal vegetables such as red peppers, courgettes and cherry tomatoes, cut into chunks

PEPPERS

Peppers can be eaten raw, dipped into mayonnaise as a crudité, grilled, baked, roasted or stewed. Although they can be picked and eaten when green, I prefer to let them ripen until they are red and sweet in flavour. These were grown in our greenhouse and provided us with a plentiful crop throughout the summer.

Ingredients

Serves 6 as an accompaniment

- 600g ripe fresh tomatoes, or one 400g tin of San Marzano plum tomatoes

- 2 tablespoons extra virgin olive oil

- 1 large onion, finely chopped

- 1 large garlic clove, crushed

- 1kg small to medium courgettes (roughly 8), sliced thinly crossways

- salt & freshly ground black pepper

COURGETTES

As any keen gardener will know, courgettes are simply immature marrows. If picked when small and tender, they have a sweet delicate flavour. We grow several varieties including 'Sarzana' and 'Spineless Beauty'.

Courgettes Provençales

Courgettes are one of the most prolific and versatile of the summer vegetables in our garden. They can be used in numerous ways – sliced, blanched and tossed into a leaf salad, coated with batter and deep fried or grilled on the barbecue. Toss them into hot cooked pasta with a little olive oil and chopped red chilli or stuff them with onions, breadcrumbs, herbs and cheese.

This recipe braises the courgettes over a slow heat with onions, garlic, tomatoes and oil – ingredients typical of Provence in southern France.

Delicious served with roast lamb or beef, Chicken wrapped with Parma Ham & Basil (see recipe p33), or Spinach & Mozzarella Tart (see recipe p27).

Method

1. Remove the skins from the tomatoes by placing them in a bowl of boiling water. After 1 minute the skins should peel off easily. Chop the tomatoes roughly and set aside.

2. Put the oil into a heavy-based saucepan and place over a moderate heat. Add the onion and garlic and allow them to soften but not brown. Add the sliced courgettes, followed by the chopped tomatoes.

3. Leave to simmer uncovered over a low heat for about 20 minutes, stirring occasionally, until the courgettes are cooked through. Remove from the heat, season to taste and drizzle with a little more olive oil. Serve hot or cold.

Couscous Salad

Couscous is pasta in its simplest form. Invented by the Berbers of northern Algeria and Morocco, it remains a staple in Northern Africa, the Middle East and Sicily. Traditionally, it is cooked in a couscoussière, a tall metal pot in which meat and vegetables are stewed, whilst the couscous sits in a steamer over the top. Couscous is made from the hardest part of the durum wheat grain, and if starting from scratch would be steamed two or three times to give it its light and fluffy texture. However, the couscous available to us in the shops has been pre-steamed and dried, needing only to be rehydrated with boiling water or stock – instant food at its best.

Delicious with Lamb Brochettes (see recipe p91), Coronation Chicken (see recipe p73), Roast Leg of Spring Lamb (see recipe p35) and Loin of Pork with Parsley Stuffing (see recipe p145).

Method

1. Heat the stock or vegetable bouillon with the saffron in a small, heavy-based pan. Allow to boil for one minute.

2. Place the couscous in a large bowl and pour the stock over the top. Cover with cling film and leave to stand undisturbed for 5 minutes – by the end of this time all the liquid should have been absorbed into the grains.

3. Gently stir the couscous with a fork, then add the onion, pepper, celery, tomatoes and herbs.

4. Finally, stir in the olive oil and lemon juice and season to taste. Serve immediately or allow to cool completely.

Ingredients

Serves 4 – 6 as an accompaniment

500ml vegetable stock (recipe p237) or vegetable bouillon

pinch of saffron strands

300g couscous

1 small red onion, finely chopped

1 small red pepper, finely chopped

1 stick of celery, finely sliced

approximately 275g small cherry or baby plum tomatoes, halved

2 tablespoons fresh herbs such as parsley, coriander and chives, chopped

2 tablespoons olive oil

1 tablespoon freshly squeezed lemon juice

salt & freshly ground black pepper

Risotto with Broad Beans & Asparagus

Marco Polo is credited with bringing rice from the Far East to Europe when he returned to Venice in 1295, having spent 20 years in China. Most of the rice used in risottos is still grown in the valley around the Po, the largest river in Italy, which flows from Piedmont to the Adriatic Sea near Venice where Marco Polo landed. There are three varieties of rice commonly used in risottos – Vialone, Carnaroli and Arborio.

Method

1. Blanch the beans and the asparagus in boiling salted water until they are just tender but still firm. Drain and set aside.

2. Using a heavy-based saucepan large enough to allow for the expansion of the rice, sauté the onion in the butter until it is soft and translucent, but not coloured. Add the rice to the pan, stirring well so that it becomes coated with butter. Next add the wine and stir well until it has completely evaporated.

3. Add a ladleful of the hot stock and bring to a simmer, stirring well. As the stock is absorbed add more, continuing in this way for approximately 18 minutes (the time will vary depending on the type of rice used), until the rice is soft and creamy but the grains are still firm in the centre – 'al dente'.

4. Stir in the prepared broad beans and asparagus, followed by about half the Parmesan cheese. Season with salt and freshly ground black pepper to taste. Serve with a generous sprinkling of the remaining Parmesan cheese.

Ingredients

Serves 6

- 125g podded tender young broad beans

- 10 asparagus spears, cut into fine slices but keeping the tip whole

- 1 medium onion, finely chopped

- large knob of butter

- 500g risotto rice

- 1 glass dry white wine

- 1½ litres hot vegetable stock (recipe p237) or vegetable bouillon

- 75g Parmesan cheese, freshly grated

- salt & freshly ground black pepper

BROAD BEANS
The first broad beans of the season are small, tender and sweet. This variety is 'Broad Fava' which will not require peeling if picked when young.

Summer Pudding

This is a quintessential English dessert made with simple ingredients. It is the perfect pudding to make when there is a glut of ripe fruit in the garden. Use any red or black summer fruits in whatever proportions you have to hand. Although this recipe is for one large pudding, it can easily be adapted to make several individual ones. Prepare it the day before you wish to serve it.

Method

1. Place the assorted fruit in a heavy-based pan together with the sugar and water and simmer for approximately 3 – 5 minutes until the fruit is soft but still retains its bright colour. Remove from the heat and tip into a sieve over a bowl to catch the juice.

2. Cut the crusts from the sliced white bread. Dip the slices of bread in the reserved juice, then use them to line the pudding basin, cutting them to shape where necessary.

3. Spoon the fruit into the bread-lined basin, then completely cover it with more bread dipped in the juice. Keep any leftover juice in a small jug.

4. Stand the basin on a tray, cover the top of the pudding with a small plate or saucer of appropriate size and place a heavy weight on the top. Leave overnight in the fridge.

5. Just before serving, remove the plate and weight. Place a serving dish upside down over the top of the pudding basin, then quickly turn them both over together. Shake sharply – this should release the pudding from the basin. Decorate with fresh fruit. To serve, pour a little of the reserved juice over each slice. Delicious with double cream or crème fraîche.

Ingredients

For a 17cm diameter,
1 litre pudding basin
Serves 6 – 8

1kg assorted summer fruits such as raspberries, strawberries, redcurrants, blackcurrants and blackberries

125g caster sugar

50ml water

10 – 12 slices of white bread, slightly stale

Cherry Clafoutis

Although it is believed that clafoutis has its origins in southern central France, this particular recipe comes from Switzerland. The French version resembles a sweet Yorkshire pudding studded with fruit, tasty of course; but 'Swiss-style', it has been transformed into a dessert of real subtlety and substance.

Sweet cherries are believed to have been brought to central Europe by the Romans where they crossed with the European wild cherry, seeding and spreading throughout the countryside. Thus, in Switzerland in the 16th century, cherries were considered a 'fruit for all', similar to wild blackberries in this country, available for anyone to pick. These days, cherry trees are more likely to be part of a mixed arable farm, particularly in the villages around Basle in north-west Switzerland where a good proportion of them will be used to make Kirsch. Although cherries are the classic ingredient, other fruits can be used – you could try redcurrants, plums, or even prunes. Whatever you use, a splash of strong alcohol makes all the difference.

Method

1. Grease a large baking dish with some of the butter. Preheat the oven to 180°C (gas mark 4). Leaving the crusts on the bread, cut it into cubes approximately 1½ - 2cm in size and place in a large bowl. Put the milk into a small pan and warm it over a low heat, then pour it evenly over the cubed bread.

2. In another bowl, beat the eggs together then add the almonds, hazelnuts, caster sugar, cinnamon, cherries, liquor and moistened bread. Mix together well and pour into the buttered baking dish.

3. Sprinkle the top with the flaked almonds and demerara sugar, then dot the surface with butter. Place in the preheated oven for approximately 30 minutes, until nicely browned on the top. Serve with pouring cream or crème fraîche.

Ingredients

Serves 8

large knob of butter

300g brioche or white bread (roughly 12 thick slices)

300ml milk

8 medium eggs

60g chopped almonds

60g chopped hazelnuts

60g caster sugar

1 level teaspoon ground cinnamon

400g griottine cherries and 8 tablespoons of the liquor (alternatively, use pitted fresh cherries, soaked in Kirsch overnight)

40g flaked almonds

60g demerara sugar

CHERRIES

Fresh, juicy cherries are not only delicious, they are also extremely good for you. They are rich in cancer-fighting antioxidants and anti-inflammatory compounds.

Pavlova

Meringues are a miracle – egg whites, sugar and copious quantities of air. Pavlovas have a small amount of cornflour and vinegar added, which gives them a delicious chewy centre.

The name comes from the famous ballerina Anna Pavlova who was best known for her interpretation of the dying swan in Tchaikovsky's Swan Lake. A good pavlova should be as delicate, light and creamy as her satin and voile tutu.

Method

1. Preheat the oven to 120°C (gas mark ¾). Cover a large baking sheet with baking parchment and mark a circle on the paper approximately 25cm in diameter. If making small pavlovas mark several circles approximately 9cm in diameter.

2. In a large metal bowl, whisk the egg whites to stiff peaks – they should form small points and hold their shape when the beater is lifted out of the bowl.

3. Gradually whisk the sugar into the egg whites, spoonful by spoonful. The mixture should start to become firm and satiny in appearance. Next gently fold the cornflour, vinegar and vanilla extract into the mixture with a metal spoon.

4. If making one large pavlova, spread half the mixture onto the circle on the baking parchment to form the base. Heap the remainder around the edge as if forming the sides of a large bowl. For small ones, divide the mixture up and, using the same process, make 8 – 10 small bowl shapes. Bake in the preheated oven for 1 hour, then turn off the oven and leave the pavlova inside to cool.

5. To serve, whip the cream to soft peaks, spread into the base of the pavlova and then fill the centre with the fresh fruit of your choice.

Ingredients

Makes one large pavlova, approximately 25cm in diameter, or 8 – 10 small ones, approximately 9cm in diameter

4 egg whites

225g caster sugar

1 level teaspoon cornflour

1 teaspoon white wine vinegar

½ teaspoon vanilla extract

200ml double cream

fresh fruit such as raspberries, strawberries or blueberries

RASPBERRIES

Raspberries are my favourite summer fruit. We grow two varieties – 'Glen Ample' which crop in the summer, and 'Autumn Bliss' which fruit well into November. Prized for their intense flavour, raspberries are also a rich source of vitamins A and C, potassium and iron.

Fresh Fruit Tartlets

These delicate pastries make pretty desserts or special treats for afternoon tea. Any fresh fruit can be used – enjoy designing your own decoration using whatever is to hand.

If you are not going to eat the tarts immediately, it is a good idea to brush the inside of the baked pastry cases with melted white chocolate before filling with crème pâtissière to prevent the pastry from softening.

Method

1. First make the sweet pastry as described on p232. Remove from the fridge and allow to almost reach room temperature. Lightly dust the work surface and rolling pin with flour, then roll the pastry out, lightly but firmly, until it is approximately 3mm thick. Line the tartlet tins with the pastry and place in the fridge to rest for at least 20 minutes. Preheat the oven to 180°C (gas mark 4).

2. When the pastry has rested, take pieces of baking parchment slightly larger than the tartlet tins. Screw them up then flatten them out again. Place one piece in the bottom of each lined tin and cover with ceramic baking beans or rice. Bake in the preheated oven for 8 - 10 minutes, then remove the baking parchment and beans and return to the oven for a further 5 - 10 minutes, until the pastry is set and golden brown. When cool, remove from the tins.

3. Meanwhile make the crème pâtissière (see recipe p244). When cool, spoon a quantity into each pastry case, making sure you leave sufficient room for the fruit.

4. Lay your choice of fruit on top of the crème pâtissière. Pile it up as much as you like, giving free rein to your artistic talents. If desired, you can sprinkle the top with icing sugar just before serving.

Ingredients

Makes 6 - 8 tartlets, depending on size and shape

500g sweet pastry
(recipe p232)

400ml crème pâtissière
(recipe p244)

fresh fruit and berries of your choice such as strawberries, raspberries, blueberries, red and blackcurrants, apricots or peaches

ALPINE STRAWBERRIES

These plants grow like weeds in our garden. The fruit is small but intensely flavoured and crops all through the summer. They are a real speciality in Italy; sadly we don't see them in the shops in Britain. Strawberries contain more vitamin C than oranges and are also a good source of potassium and folic acid.

Vanilla Ice Cream

The best ice cream is made with a 'custard'. The addition of egg yolks gives it a velvety texture and superb flavour. This recipe can also be used as a base to which fruit and other flavours can be added. As only the yolks of the eggs are needed, save the whites to make a Pavlova (see recipe p101) or Langue du Chat Biscuits (see recipe overleaf).

If you do not have an ice cream maker, don't worry. You can achieve a satisfactory result by stirring the mixture from time to time as it freezes. It will keep for 2 - 3 weeks in the freezer.

Method

1. Pour the single cream into a saucepan. Add the vanilla pod and bring to the boil. Remove from the heat, split the vanilla pod down the side and scrape out the seeds with a sharp knife. Add them to the hot cream.

2. Place the egg yolks in a large heatproof bowl. Pour the hot single cream onto the yolks whilst beating them vigorously. Stir in the caster sugar.

3. Set the bowl over a pan of simmering water, stirring the egg and cream mixture until it thickens to a custard. Take care not to cook it too quickly or you will end up with scrambled egg. If any lumps appear, use a small hand whisk to break them up. Set aside to cool.

4. In another bowl, whisk the double cream to soft peaks, then gently fold into the custard.

5. Pour into your ice cream maker, or alternatively into a metal bowl, and place in the freezer, stirring several times as it freezes.

6. Serve with fresh fruit, raspberry sauce (see recipe p242), chocolate sauce (see recipe p243) or toffee sauce (see recipe p242). Delicious with Langue du Chat Biscuits (see recipe overleaf).

Ingredients

Serves 6 - 8

400ml single cream

1 vanilla pod

6 large egg yolks

100g caster sugar

400ml double cream

VANILLA

Vanilla pods are the fruit of the Vanilla Orchid, native to central and northern South America. The fresh pod is full of thousands of tiny seeds which intensify in flavour during the drying and curing process. Vanilla pods are the second most expensive flavouring in the world, after saffron.

Ingredients

Makes approximately 30

4 egg whites

110g ground almonds

110g caster sugar

2 heaped teaspoons plain white flour

Langue du Chat Biscuits

Literally translated these are 'cat's tongue' biscuits – the name refers to the shape. Traditionally they are served with ice cream. This recipe is a perfect way to use up any leftover egg whites. The biscuits can be made in advance and stored in an airtight container for up to 1 week.

Method

1. Preheat the oven to 150°C (gas mark 2). Line a large baking sheet with baking parchment. In a large bowl, beat the egg whites until firm.

2. In a second bowl, mix the ground almonds, sugar and flour together, then fold lightly into the beaten egg whites.

3. Using a piping bag, pipe the mixture onto the lined baking sheet in the shape of 'cats tongues' roughly 7cm in length. Alternatively, spoon into small rounds.

4. Bake in the preheated oven for approximately 15 minutes, until firm and golden. When cool enough to handle, peel off the baking parchment and leave to cool completely on a cooling rack.

Summer Fruit Jam

Ingredients

equal quantities of fruit and sugar – check overleaf to see if lemon juice should be added and the type of sugar that should be used

The process of jam-making is extremely therapeutic and very straightforward if you follow a few simple rules. As autumn approaches a store cupboard lined with jars of home-made jams will enable you to enjoy the flavours of summer right through the chilly winter months.

For jam to be a success, there must be a balance between acidity, pectin and sugar. Some fruits contain more acid than others – this is usually quite obvious as they are rather tart when tasted. If necessary, lemon juice can be added to raise the acidity level.

Pectin is present in all fruit and is needed to set the jam. Fruits with a low pectin level should be made with preserving or jam sugar that contains added pectin. If the fruit is high in pectin, use granulated sugar. This prevents the jam from setting too soon, allowing it to cook properly and develop its flavour fully.

Most jam recipes require equal weights of fruit and sugar. Taking into account the natural sugar present in the fruit, this will produce a jam with a total sugar content of roughly 60%, which should keep for up to 3 years. Jams with a lower sugar content need to be eaten within 6 months.

Before starting to make the jam, sterilise your jam jars:

1. Preheat the oven to 180°C (gas mark 4).

2. Wash the jars and lids in hot soapy water, then rinse. Do not dry with a tea towel.

3. Place the jars and lids on a baking sheet and leave in the oven for at least 10 minutes. Allow to cool slightly before filling with hot jam.

Summer Fruit Jam

Method

1. Remember to sterilise your jars and lids (see p107).

2. Pick the fruit over to remove any with blemishes and wash if necessary. Remove any stones from the centre of the fruit. These can be tied in a piece of muslin and added to the jam as it is boiling to help with setting.

3. Layer the fruit and sugar in a large, heavy-based pan and if possible leave overnight. This will draw the juice out of the fruit and start to dissolve the sugar. If short of time, you can soften the fruit over a low heat before adding the sugar, but do not allow the mixture to boil before the sugar has completely dissolved.

4. Add lemon juice if required and place over a moderate heat. Bring to a rolling boil, stirring occasionally. When the mixture has started to thicken and look like jam (usually between 10 and 20 minutes, depending on the fruit used), test for setting. If using a sugar thermometer, be sure to warm it up before you plunge it into the boiling jam. Setting point is 105°C/220°F. If you do not have a thermometer, place a plate in the refrigerator for a few minutes. Spoon a small quantity of jam mixture onto the cold plate and return to the fridge to cool for a moment or two. The jam will be at setting point if it wrinkles when you push it with your finger.

5. Skim any scum off the surface of the jam and leave to cool for approximately 10 minutes before pouring into the sterilised jars. Cover with a waxed disc, wax side down, then seal with the lids whilst still hot to allow a vacuum to form. Cool for 24 hours before labelling and storing in a cool, dark place.

Strawberries

Acidity level: low – add lemon juice
(2 tablespoons per 500g fruit)

Pectin level: low – use preserving or jam sugar

Raspberries

Acidity level: medium – no lemon juice needed

Pectin level: medium to low – use preserving or jam sugar

Redcurrants & blackcurrants

Acidity level: high – no lemon juice needed

Pectin level: high – use granulated sugar

Cherries

Acidity level: medium – lemon juice only needed if very ripe
(2 teaspoons per 500g of fruit)

Pectin level: low – use preserving or jam sugar

Damsons & plums

Acidity level: high – no lemon juice needed

Pectin level: high – use granulated sugar

Blackberries

Acidity level: medium – no lemon juice needed

Pectin level: medium – use either granulated
or preserving or jam sugar

Carrot Cake

Unlike many carrot cakes which are made with oil, this Swiss version is beautifully light and moist. It is fat free and can easily be made gluten free by substituting the small amount of flour in the recipe with more ground almonds. Conversely, by substituting the ground almonds with more flour, it can be made nut free. It is important to grate the carrots very finely otherwise they will not melt into the mixture as the cake bakes. For best results, allow it to mature for a day or two before eating. It also freezes very well.

I like to decorate this cake very simply by dredging it with icing sugar or covering the top with lemon water icing (see recipe overleaf).

Method

1. Line the sides and base of a 23cm diameter loose-bottomed cake tin or two 1kg loaf tins, with baking parchment. Use a little melted butter underneath the parchment to help keep it in place. Preheat the oven to 160°C (gas mark 2½).

2. In a large mixing bowl whisk together the egg yolks and one half of the sugar until thick, pale and doubled in volume. Take care not to add the sugar to the yolks until you are ready to start whisking or they will begin to coagulate.

3. Fold in the carrots, ground almonds, lemon zest and juice. When well combined, stir in the flour and baking powder. The mixture will be quite stiff at this stage.

4. In another bowl, whisk the egg whites and salt together until they keep their shape. Add the remaining sugar, bit by bit, and continue whisking until the mixture is thick and glossy. Gently fold into the cake mixture spoonful by spoonful, taking care not to knock the air out of the egg whites.

Ingredients

For one 23cm diameter cake or two 1kg loaves

- 5 large eggs, separated
- 250g caster sugar, divided into two portions of 125g each
- 250g carrots, peeled and finely grated
- 250g ground almonds
- grated zest and juice of 1 lemon
- 75g plain white flour
- 2 teaspoons baking powder
- pinch of salt
- icing sugar or Lemon Water Icing (recipe overleaf) to decorate

CARROTS

One of the most versatile vegetables in the kitchen, carrots are equally delicious eaten raw or cooked. They contain a very high quantity of vitamin A which is beneficial for retinal function – hence the belief that eating carrots helps night vision.

Carrot Cake

Ingredients

For one 23cm diameter cake
or two 1kg loaves

140g icing sugar

**4 dessertspoons freshly
squeezed lemon juice**

**finely grated zest of 2
lemons**

5. Pour into the prepared cake tins and bake in the preheated oven for approximately 35 – 40 minutes, until risen and firm to the touch. To check that it is baked, pierce the centre of the cake with a thin skewer – it should come out clean.

6. Allow to stand for a few minutes before removing from the tin. Leave to cool on a cooling rack, the cake will sink a little at this stage. To decorate, dust liberally with icing sugar or cover with lemon water icing.

Lemon Water Icing

Method

1. Place the icing sugar in a mixing bowl. Add the lemon juice and zest and beat well until combined.

2. Spread over the surface of the cake evenly with a palette knife and leave for several hours to set.

Limoncello

This recipe comes from the romantic area of Italy known as the Amalfi coast. It is a region of huge contrasts with vertiginous cliffs plunging steeply into the sea, lemon groves clinging to every ledge. I climbed the coastal paths from Ravello to Positano in late May when the scent of the lemon blossom was totally intoxicating. Limoncello is a refreshing liqueur made by steeping lemon zest in alcohol.

For best results, use organic lemons. Buy the strongest vodka you can find – I use a Polish vodka which is 160° proof (80% alcohol by volume). The high alcohol percentage prevents the limoncello from turning to ice in the freezer.

This is a very biblical recipe, with an interval of 40 days and 40 nights between each of the stages. Although the limoncello can be drunk at the end of the second stage, the longer it is left to mature, the more delicious it will be.

Store your limoncello in the freezer and bring it out just before serving – it won't freeze because of the high sugar and alcohol content. Also, chill the liqueur glasses in advance.

Limoncello is also delicious drizzled on fresh strawberries.

Method

1. Carefully pare the peel from the lemons with a sharp knife, ensuring the white pith is left behind.

2. Pour the vodka into a large glass jar, then add the peeled lemon zest. Cover with the lid and leave in a cool dark place for 40 days. Gradually, the vodka will absorb the flavour and rich colour of the lemon zest. At the end of this stage the zest will be pale and quite brittle – this is a sign that you can progress to the next stage.

3. Put the water and sugar in a heavy-based saucepan and place over a low heat, stirring well until the sugar is completely dissolved. Bring to boil for approximately 5 minutes, then remove from the heat and leave to cool.

Ingredients

Makes approximately 1½ litres

8 organic unwaxed lemons

750ml 160° proof vodka

625ml water

500g caster sugar

Limoncello

4. When the sugar syrup has cooled to room temperature, add it to the vodka and lemon zest in the glass jar. Don't worry if it looks slightly cloudy at this stage. Return to a cool dark place for a further 40 days.

5. Finally, remove as much lemon zest as possible with a slotted spoon. Pour the limoncello through a strainer lined with moistened muslin and decant into bottles. Store in the freezer until ready to serve.

THE AMALFI COAST

This beautiful coastline is the home of Limoncello. The steep mountainsides are covered with terraces to provide a foothold for the lemon groves, which thrive in the rich, volcanic soil.

Fresh Lemonade

Old-fashioned, fresh lemonade is a wonderfully refreshing summer drink, perfect for al fresco meals. This recipe makes a concentrated syrup that will keep for 4 weeks in the fridge. It can also be stored in plastic bottles in the freezer.

Method

1. Carefully pare the peel from the lemons with a sharp knife, ensuring the white pith is left behind.

2. Halve the lemons and squeeze thoroughly.

3. Place the water, lemon juice, lemon zest and caster sugar in a large, heavy-based pan. Bring to the boil and simmer gently for 15 minutes. Remove from the heat and leave to cool for 1 hour. If left any longer the syrup will become bitter.

4. Strain through a fine sieve and transfer to bottles for storage.

5. To serve, dilute with sparkling or still water – 5 parts of water to 1 part lemon syrup.

Ingredients

Makes approximately 1½ litres of syrup, before diluting

12 organic unwaxed lemons

500ml water

850g caster sugar

LEMONS

I have been growing lemons at home for at least 10 years. They overwinter indoors and stand outside from the end of May until late September. This variety is 'Meyer' which is particularly sweet and juicy with a thin skin – perfect for making lemonade.

Autumn

Recipes

Beetroot Soup

My childhood memories of beetroot are of bitter, vinegary pickled chunks served up at school dinners. Since I've grown up, I have discovered that there are many other wonderful ways to use this colourful and nutritious root vegetable.

Method

1. Heat the oil in a heavy-based saucepan and add the onion and garlic. Allow to soften but not colour.

2. Add the beetroots, carrot, celery, tomato, rice and a little salt and pepper, and cover with the stock. Bring to the boil and simmer gently until the vegetables are tender – approximately 10 - 15 minutes.

3. Allow to cool slightly, then purée using either an electric hand blender, liquidiser or food processor.

4. To serve, reheat gently and adjust the seasoning. Top each portion with a swirl of soured cream and a sprinkling of parsley.

Ingredients

Serves 6

1 tablespoon sunflower oil

1 small onion, finely chopped

1 garlic clove, crushed

500g fresh beetroots, peeled and chopped

1 carrot, finely sliced

1 small stick of celery, finely sliced

1 tomato, skinned and chopped

1 tablespoon basmati rice

salt & freshly ground black pepper

1.2 litres vegetable stock (recipe p237) or vegetable bouillon

soured cream

fresh parsley, chopped

BEETROOTS

Beetroots contain more sucrose than any other vegetable. They are also a rich source of antioxidants – helpful in the fight against cancer.

Pumpkin-seed Bread

This recipe is based on a moist, crusty loaf I love to eat when on holiday in Switzerland. The seeds give it a tasty, nutty flavour and interesting texture. Delicious with Beetroot Soup (see recipe p121) or Mushroom Pâté (see recipe p125).

Method

1. Place the white and rye flour in a large mixing bowl together with the salt and butter. Rub the butter into the flour until the mixture resembles fine breadcrumbs.

2. In a small jug, dissolve the yeast in the tepid water. Make a well in the centre of the flour mixture and pour in the yeast and water, followed by the milk. Gradually draw the flour away from the sides of the bowl into the centre to combine with the liquids, forming a dough.

3. Remove the dough from the bowl and knead on a lightly floured surface for approximately 8 minutes until it is smooth and elastic. Spread the dough out and place the pumpkin seeds in the centre. Continue kneading until the seeds are evenly distributed and the dough becomes smooth again.

4. Divide the dough into two pieces, 400g each in weight, mould into balls, cover with a clean tea towel and leave to rest for 5 minutes.

5. Roll each ball into a sausage roughly 30cm in length, fatter in the middle and tapering at each end, then curl it into a crescent shape. Lay the loaves on a tray lined with baking parchment. Dust with a little flour, cover with a clean tea towel and leave in a warm place to prove for approximately 1½ hours. They will be ready when they have doubled in size and the dough springs back slowly when pressed. Preheat the oven to 200°C (gas mark 6).

6. Bake in the preheated oven for approximately 25 minutes, until golden brown. To test whether they are ready, tap the bottom of the loaves – they should sound hollow.

Ingredients

Makes 2 loaves

240g strong white flour

240g light rye flour

10g sea salt

20g butter

15g fresh yeast (or 8g dried yeast)

135ml tepid water

135ml milk

140g pumpkin seeds

PUMPKIN SEEDS

Pumpkin seeds are a rich source of nutrients (including magnesium, manganese, phosphorous, iron, copper, protein, zinc and monosaturated fats), and also possess anti-inflammatory properties to help reduce levels of cholesterol in the blood.

Toasted, they can be sprinkled on top of a leaf salad to give flavour and bite. To prepare your own, rinse the fresh seeds under running water, pat them dry and spread out on a baking tray. Place in a moderate oven for a few minutes until dry and slightly crispy.

Mushroom Pâté

Freshly picked mushrooms are one of autumn's greatest pleasures. This rich and tasty pâté is delicious with toast or as a filling for Parmesan Choux Puffs (see recipe p72).

Method

1. Melt the knob of butter in a medium-sized heavy-based saucepan, then add the shallots and garlic. Cook for several minutes until soft but not coloured.

2. Add the mushrooms, nutmeg, salt and freshly ground black pepper. Cook over a moderate heat until the juice from the mushrooms has almost evaporated. Pour in the wine and continue to cook until it has also evaporated. Transfer to a bowl and allow to cool.

3. When completely cold, process with a hand blender – the texture should remain quite coarse. Finally, stir in the crème fraîche and cream cheese and mix together thoroughly. Check the seasoning, transfer to a bowl and leave in the fridge for several hours to set.

Ingredients

Serves 4 - 5

large knob of butter

2 medium shallots, finely chopped

1 garlic clove, crushed

200g fresh field, portobello or chestnut mushrooms, wiped and roughly chopped

pinch of freshly grated nutmeg

salt & freshly ground black pepper

1 tablespoon dry white wine

75g crème fraîche

100g cream cheese

WILD MUSHROOMS

Field mushrooms are a truly seasonal crop, only appearing in autumn when the weather conditions are perfect.

Fig Salad

This is the simplest and most scrumptious of salads. It is essential to use really ripe fruit – once picked, an unripe fig will never ripen. Test the fruit by squeezing it gently – it should yield but not disintegrate.

Fig trees are quite hardy and will produce vast quantities of fruit if grown against a south-facing garden wall – even in Yorkshire. Arrange the salad on a large platter if serving as a main course. Alternatively, serve on individual plates as a starter.

Method

1. Lightly wipe each fig with a clean damp cloth, then cut a cross in the top of each one. Gently squeeze the bases so that the tops open out, exposing the flesh of the fruit. Spread the rocket leaves on a serving plate and arrange the figs on top.

2. Lay the slices of Parma ham in between the figs, together with the mozzarella. Scatter the lemon zest over the top, season with black pepper, then drizzle with a little freshly squeezed lemon juice and extra virgin olive oil. Serve with crusty bread.

Ingredients

Per person

2 ripe figs

handful of rocket leaves

2 slices of Parma ham

2 or 3 slices of buffalo mozzarella cheese, torn

lemon zest, freshly grated

freshly ground black pepper

freshly squeezed lemon juice

extra virgin olive oil

FIGS

Ripe figs have delicate rose-coloured flesh and a sweet musky flavour. Rich in calcium, potassium, phosphorus and iron, they have one of the highest combined mineral counts of any cultivated fruit and are also a valuable source of dietary fibre.

Mushrooms in Wine & Cream

This versatile recipe can be served in numerous different ways. For a hot starter, spoon it into individual ramekins and serve with soldiers of toast. Try it as a tasty filling for Pancakes (see recipe p43), a rich creamy sauce for pasta, a vegetarian topping for Rösti (see recipe p155), or as a delicious mushroom stroganoff, served with fluffy rice.

Method

1. Preheat the oven to 150°C (gas mark 2). Slice the bread into thick rounds, brush each side with a little olive oil and place on a baking tray in the oven for a few minutes. When they have dried out a little and turned golden, remove and set aside.

2. Melt half the butter in a medium-sized heavy-based saucepan over a moderate heat. Add the onion and cook for a few minutes, stirring occasionally, until soft but not coloured. Pour in the wine, stir well and allow to boil rapidly. Once the liquid has reduced by a half, stir in the double cream and continue to cook until the cream has reduced and the sauce is thick enough to coat the back of a wooden spoon.

3. Meanwhile, melt the remaining butter in a large, heavy-based saucepan over a moderate heat. Add the mushrooms, season with salt and freshly ground black pepper and cook, stirring well, until all the juices from the mushrooms have evaporated. Add the cooked mushrooms to the onion, wine and cream, check the seasoning and simmer for four or five minutes.

4. Preheat the grill. To serve, place the prepared rounds of bread in individual ovenproof dishes. Cover with a generous quantity of mushrooms and cream, sprinkle with the grated cheese and grill until golden and bubbling. Garnish with fresh parsley.

Ingredients

Serves 5 - 6

- a loaf of crusty bread which will easily cut into rounds
- a little olive oil
- 100g butter
- 1 onion, finely chopped
- 400ml dry white wine
- 250ml double cream
- 900g small mushrooms, wild or button, finely sliced
- salt & freshly ground black pepper
- 80g raclette or Gruyère cheese, grated
- 2 tablespoons fresh parsley, chopped

Swiss Onion Tart

Onions are a staple of Swiss cooking, with their own special festival, the Zibelemärit, held in Bern on the last Monday in November each year. The story goes that during the terrible fire of 1405 when the city burned down, the neighbouring market gardeners rallied round and helped to vanquish the flames. In return they were given the right to sell their onions in the city every year.

This is a very simple recipe which relies on the onions being prepared carefully. They must be cooked slowly over a moderate heat so that they soften and caramelise, releasing their natural sugars.

Method

1. First make the pastry as described on p233. Remove from the fridge and allow to almost reach room temperature. Lightly dust the work surface and your rolling pin with flour and begin to roll out the pastry lightly but firmly. Keep turning it and dusting the work surface to prevent it from sticking and continue until the pastry is larger than your tart case and approximately 3mm thick. Roll it around the rolling pin and lift it onto the tart case. Gently coax it down the sides, making sure it isn't stretched. Trim off the excess with a sharp knife and place in the fridge to rest for at least 20 minutes.

2. Meanwhile, make the filling. Put the onions, butter, salt and freshly ground black pepper into a wide, heavy-based pan (ideally a sauteuse pan). Place over a moderate heat, and stew for approximately 30 minutes, stirring occasionally, until the onions are soft and golden in colour and are beginning to caramelise. Set aside to cool.

3. Preheat the oven to 180°C (gas mark 4). When the pastry has rested, take a piece of baking parchment a little larger than the tart case, screw it into a ball, then flatten it out over the surface of the pastry.

Ingredients

For a 28cm fluted tart case
Serves 8

425g simple shortcrust pastry (recipe p233)

1kg onions, finely sliced

25g butter

salt & freshly ground black pepper

3 large eggs

200ml whipping cream

Swiss Onion Tart

4. Cover the top with ceramic baking beans or rice. Bake in the preheated oven for 10 minutes, then remove the paper and beans and return to the oven for a further 10 minutes, until set and golden. Remove from the oven and set aside to cool. Increase the temperature of the oven to 200°C (gas mark 6).

5. In a jug, whisk together the eggs and cream with a little more salt and pepper. Place the prebaked pastry case onto a baking tray and fill with the prepared onions. Slide out the oven shelf halfway, ensuring it is still secure and level, and place the tray and tart on the shelf. Pour the egg and cream mixture carefully over the top of the onions. This avoids having to carry the full tart to the oven, risking spilling the mixture over the sides of the pastry, which will make it stick.

6. Bake the tart in the preheated oven for approximately 30 – 35 minutes, until set and golden brown but not risen. Serve warm, with a leaf salad and new potatoes.

ONIONS

Onions are the most flavoursome vegetable in the kitchen – it is impossible to imagine making soups, stews or casseroles without them. Harvested in autumn, they are laid in trays for the tops to dry so they can be kept through the winter. Brown onions have a stronger flavour than red onions, which are mild and sweet.

Roasted Pumpkins with Cheese Fondue

The soft orange flesh of the pumpkin and the rich, creamy texture of cheese fondue are a superb combination. Served with slices of crusty bread this is a hearty main course dish. Cheese fondue was traditionally eaten in Swiss mountain villages where fresh food was scarce during the winter months. Forced to rely on their own reserves of wine and cheese the resourceful Swiss combined the two and fondue was invented. It is normally prepared in a communal pot, a 'caquelon', with each person using their own fork to dip cubes of bread into the melted cheese. The caquelon sits over a spirit burner to keep the cheese bubbling slowly. If you wish to serve cheese fondue in the traditional way, use the recipe below allowing 75g Gruyère and 75g Emmental per person.

The cheese should be well matured and coarsely grated. Use a dry white wine such as a Riesling or a Chablis – the acidity helps to melt the cheese. Prepare the fondue over a very low heat in a thick-bottomed pan to prevent the cheese from burning. If the fondue curdles, add a few more drops of lemon juice.

Ingredients

Serves 4

4 small fresh pumpkins, approximately 12cm in diameter

For the fondue

1 garlic clove, cut in half

300ml dry white wine

1 teaspoon freshly squeezed lemon juice

300g Gruyère cheese, coarsely grated

300g Emmental cheese, coarsely grated

2 heaped teaspoons cornflour

2 tablespoons Kirsch

salt & freshly ground black pepper

freshly grated nutmeg

Method

1. Preheat the oven to 200°C (gas mark 6). First prepare the pumpkins. Wash them and slice off the tops keeping the stalks intact – these will serve as lids. Scrape out the stringy flesh containing the seeds and discard. You can reserve the seeds, rinse them and toast them in the oven for use in salads and other recipes (see p123).

2. Stand the pumpkins complete with lids on a baking tray lined with foil and place in the preheated oven for approximately 20 - 30 minutes, until the pumpkin flesh is tender when prodded with a knife – take care not to pierce the skin.

Roasted Pumpkins with Cheese Fondue

SWISS CHEESE

Gruyère and Emmental are the Swiss cheeses most commonly found in Britain. The canny Swiss keep the best for themselves – the Alpkäse and Bergkäse (mountain cheeses), made on the Alp with raw milk from cows whose only fodder is fresh lush grass and wild flowers, never get to this country. There are hundreds of different Swiss cheeses varying in texture and flavour – I had a hand in making the ones in this photograph in a tiny dairy on an Alp in the Engadine.

3. While the pumpkins are roasting, make the fondue. Rub the inside of a heavy-based pan with the cut side of the garlic. Pour the wine and lemon juice into the pan and heat slowly so that they do not evaporate. Add the coarsely grated cheese gradually, stirring continuously in a figure of eight motion.

4. Mix the cornflour and Kirsch together in a small jug. When the cheese is bubbling, add the Kirsch mixture slowly, stirring well until the fondue thickens. Continue to cook over a low heat for 2 - 3 minutes, constantly stirring. Season with salt, freshly ground black pepper and nutmeg to taste, then pour into the hot pumpkins.

5. Cover the pumpkins with their lids and place them back in the hot oven for a further 5 minutes. Serve with slices of crusty bread.

Haddock & Prawn Pie

This is real comfort food. Soft, flaky haddock and small tender North Sea prawns coated in a delicate creamy sauce. The dish can be finished in a number of different ways – my favourite topping is a layer of Rösti potato crisped in the oven. Buttery mashed potato or a mixture of breadcrumbs and cheese also work very well.

If you want to get ahead, prepare the fish and sauce in advance. To complete the dish, combine them together in a heavy-based saucepan and reheat thoroughly. Transfer the mixture to a gratin or pie dish and cover with the topping of your choice.

Method

1. Preheat the oven to 200°C (gas mark 6). Place the haddock fillets in the bottom of a medium-sized roasting tin. Tuck the bay leaves and the two halves of the onion in between the pieces of fish. Sprinkle with salt and pepper, cover with the milk and place in the oven for 10 - 12 minutes until the haddock is just cooked through – the time will vary depending on the thickness of the fish fillets. Remove from the oven and leave to cool for a few minutes.

2. Lift the fish out of the milk, check for bones, and set aside. Pass the milk through a sieve into a jug, discarding the bay leaves and onion. Keep it to one side for the sauce.

3. Place the prawns in a sieve and rinse with cold water. Lay on kitchen paper to dry.

4. Melt the butter in a large, heavy-based saucepan over a low heat. Add the flour, stirring constantly, allowing it to cook for a couple of minutes. Remove from the heat and add the wine, incorporating it into the flour and butter. Return to the heat and cook for several more minutes, stirring well.

Ingredients

Serves 4 - 5

For the haddock & prawn in wine & cream sauce

700g skinless haddock fillets

2 bay leaves

1 onion, cut in half

salt & freshly ground black pepper

400ml milk

400g North Sea prawns

25g butter

25g plain white flour

75ml dry white wine

200ml double cream

For the topping

100g grated Gruyère cheese and 100g breadcrumbs, mixed together

or

1 quantity of Rösti potato mix (recipe p155)

or

1 quantity of Buttery Mashed Potato (recipe p194)

Haddock & Prawn Pie

5. Remove from the heat again and add the reserved milk in stages. Stir well and return to the heat, allowing it to cook gently for two more minutes. Remove from the heat and stir in the double cream.

6. Add the reserved haddock to the sauce, followed by the prawns. Stir well to break up any large pieces of fish. Check the seasoning, adding more if required.

7. Place the saucepan back on the low heat, stirring well, until the contents are piping hot. Transfer to a gratin or pie dish and cover with the topping of your choice. Place in the preheated oven or under the grill for a few minutes until golden brown on top. Serve with crisp, green seasonal vegetables.

BAY LEAVES

These are the glossy, slightly leathery leaves of the Bay Laurel tree commonly found in the Mediterranean. They give a delicate flavour to stocks, soups, stews and casseroles and are one of the ingredients of the classic 'bouquet garni'. Bay trees grow well in England and we have several in our garden. To preserve the leaves by drying, tie them in bunches and hang in a warm, well ventilated place for several days.

Pumpkin & Rosemary Risotto

This risotto is a real autumnal treat. Although delicate in colour, it is full of flavour. Risotto is a speciality of northern Italy where it is often served in crispy Parmesan Baskets which can be made in advance (see recipe overleaf).

Pumpkins are easy to grow, although they do tend to rampage through the vegetable garden, demanding more space than is reasonable.

Method

1. Heat the oil and a third of the butter in a medium-sized heavy-based saucepan. Add the garlic, whole sprigs of rosemary and pumpkin and cook over a low heat for about 20 minutes, stirring occasionally, until the pumpkin softens and becomes pulpy. Remove the sprigs of rosemary, then set the cooked pumpkin aside.

2. In another heavy-based saucepan, or sauteuse pan, large enough to allow for the expansion of the rice, sauté the onion in the remaining butter until soft and translucent. Add the rice, stirring well, so that it becomes coated with the butter. Next add the wine, stirring again until it has been completely absorbed.

3. Add a ladleful of the vegetable stock and bring to a simmer, then add the pumpkin mixture and half of the chopped rosemary. As the stock is absorbed add more, continuing in this way for approximately 18 minutes, (the time will vary depending on the type of rice used), until the rice is soft and creamy but the grains are still firm in the centre. Stir constantly so that the rice does not stick to the pan. You may not need to use all of the stock – it will depend on the juiciness of the pumpkin.

4. Add half of the Parmesan cheese together with the remaining chopped rosemary and season to taste. Serve with a generous sprinkling of Parmesan cheese.

Ingredients

Serves 6

- 2 tablespoons extra virgin olive oil
- 120g butter
- 1 garlic clove, crushed
- 1 dessertspoon fresh rosemary, finely chopped, plus 2 large whole sprigs
- 800g pumpkin flesh, chopped into small cubes roughly 1½cm in size
- 1 medium onion, finely chopped
- 500g risotto rice, (Vialone, Carnaroli or Arborio)
- 1 glass dry white wine
- 1½ litres hot vegetable stock (recipe p237) or vegetable bouillon
- 75g Parmesan cheese, freshly grated
- salt & freshly ground black pepper

Ingredients

Per basket

30g fresh Parmesan cheese, finely grated

Parmesan Baskets

A portion of risotto served in a home-made Parmesan basket looks and tastes very special. The baskets can be made several hours in advance and should stay crisp. If, however, they do soften, put them back over the bowl on which they were moulded and place on a baking tray in a hot oven for 3 - 4 minutes. They will crisp up again and reshape themselves.

Method

1. You will need a small ovenproof bowl of the appropriate size to hold a portion of risotto, about 12cm in diameter and 6cm deep.

2. Cut a circle of baking parchment the same size as the base of a non-stick frying pan. Lay it in the pan, cover it evenly with grated Parmesan and place over a moderate heat. When the Parmesan begins to bubble and turn golden remove the pan from the heat and allow it to cool for a few moments.

3. Whilst still hot, position it over the base of the upturned bowl. The Parmesan disc should peel away from the parchment and mould itself around the bowl. Leave to cool completely before removing. Fill with risotto just before serving.

Aubergines Parmigiana

This recipe comes from the Neapolitan area of Italy where Vesuvius, the volcano which erupted in AD79 destroying Pompeii and Herculaneum, dominates the skyline. In between the cliffs and the volcanic peaks the plains are blessed with rich, fertile soil, full of minerals deposited by the molten lava. Add hot sunshine, and the conditions are perfect for growing fruit and vegetables.

Wonderful tomatoes are produced here – 'San Marzano', an elegant plum variety which has D.O.P. status and 'Vesuviano', a cherry tomato, bursting with flavour, grown on the slopes of Vesuvius itself. Aubergines, with their long, glossy purple fruit are grown in the market gardens, and close by, in Caserta and Salerno, herds of water buffalo provide the best quality mozzarella cheese in the world. This dish is the perfect combination of all three local ingredients.

Aubergines Parmigiana is a wonderful vegetarian main course, and is also delicious as an accompaniment to roast meat. It can be made in advance and freezes very well.

Method

1. First make the tomato sauce. In a large, heavy-based saucepan, sweat the onions and garlic in a little of the oil until they are translucent but not coloured. Add the tomatoes, tomato purée, sugar, wine vinegar, oregano, basil, bay leaves and seasoning. Allow to simmer over a gentle heat for approximately 45 minutes, until thick and fragrant. Remove from the heat and set aside.

2. Whilst the sauce is simmering prepare the aubergines. Slice them into rings roughly 1½cm in width. Sprinkle liberally with salt and leave for at least ½ hour in a colander. This will draw out moisture and bitterness. Rinse the aubergines in fresh water and pat dry with kitchen paper.

Ingredients

Serves 4 – 6

- 2 medium onions, finely chopped
- 2 garlic cloves, crushed
- extra virgin olive oil
- 1kg fresh plum or Italian tinned tomatoes, skinned and chopped
- 3 tablespoons tomato purée
- 2 teaspoons sugar
- 2 tablespoons red wine vinegar
- 2 teaspoons dried oregano
- handful of fresh basil leaves, chopped
- 4 bay leaves
- salt & freshly ground black pepper
- 1kg (approximately 3 large) aubergines
- 400g mozzarella cheese, sliced thinly
- 150g Parmesan cheese, freshly grated

Aubergines Parmigiana

3. Preheat the oven to 180°C (gas mark 4). Heat 2 or 3 tablespoons of olive oil in a heavy-based frying pan. Fry the aubergines on both sides until browned and slightly crispy. Repeat, adding more oil as required until all the aubergines have been prepared.

4. To assemble, cover the bottom of a large (roughly 28 x 24cm) ovenproof dish with a layer of prepared aubergines. Next add a layer of mozzarella cheese followed by tomato sauce and a sprinkling of Parmesan cheese. Continue to fill the dish in this way, finishing with tomato sauce and plenty of Parmesan.

5. Bake in the preheated oven for approximately 40 - 45 minutes until bubbling and browned.

AUBERGINES

Originally from Asia, aubergines are these days considered a native to the Mediterranean where they are used in many regional dishes. They come in many shapes, sizes and colours from white through green to black. The most common varieties found in this country tend to be long and glossy purple in colour. These were grown in our greenhouse in Harrogate.

Loin of Pork with Parsley Stuffing

Boned loin of pork, stuffed with parsley, onion and breadcrumbs and covered with crispy crackling is one of my family's favourite meals. The recipe for the stuffing is my mother's and is equally delicious as a herb crust for pork tenderloin.

Unless you are very experienced with a boning knife, ask the butcher to remove the bones for you.

Method

1. First make the stuffing. Melt the butter in a large, heavy-based saucepan. Add the onions and cook over a gentle heat until they are translucent but not coloured. Remove from the heat, stir in the breadcrumbs and parsley, then season with salt and freshly ground black pepper. Set aside to cool.

2. Preheat the oven to 200°C (gas mark 6). Lay the boned loin of pork on the work surface skin side down. Spoon the stuffing along the centre of the piece of meat, then roll it as tightly as possible, securing it with five or six pieces of string. Tie these around the outside of the meat so that you have a parcel which looks like a large sausage roll. Any leftover stuffing will freeze very well.

3. Make sure the skin is well scored with a sharp knife at roughly 5 - 6mm intervals, then rub it with oil and salt.

4. Lay the meat on a rack in a large roasting tin and place in the preheated oven. The total roasting time will depend on the weight of the stuffed loin. Allow 33 minutes per 500g, plus an extra 30 minutes. After 30 minutes, turn the oven down to 190°C (gas mark 5).

5. Once the pork is cooked remove the meat from the roasting tin and place on a serving dish. To check, pierce with a fork – it will be ready if the juices run clear. Leave to rest in a warm place for 20 minutes before serving.

Ingredients

Serves 8

boned loin of pork, approximately 2kg in weight

sunflower or olive oil

salt

For the stuffing

160g butter

2 large onions, finely chopped

150g breadcrumbs

6 heaped tablespoons fresh parsley, chopped

salt & freshly ground black pepper

For the gravy

2 tablespoons plain white flour

300ml vegetable stock (recipe p237) or vegetable bouillon

145

Loin of Pork with Parsley Stuffing

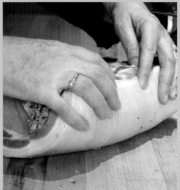

6. To make the gravy, pour away and discard all but two tablespoons of the fat from the roasting tin, retaining as much of the juice from the meat as possible. Add the flour, stir well and cook over a low heat for a couple of minutes. Remove from the heat, add the stock and mix well. Return to the heat and bring slowly to the boil, stirring constantly to incorporate the meat juices from the bottom of the roasting tin. Simmer for 5 minutes, then season to taste and strain into a gravy boat.

Delicious with Crab Apple & Quince Jelly (see recipe p171), Potato & Celeriac Dauphinoise (see recipe p192), Casseroled Red Cabbage (see recipe p204), Stewed Leeks (see p203), or Puy Lentils with Rosemary & Chilli (see recipe p189).

Lamb & Chickpea Stew with Saffron Rice

This delicious, warming lamb stew is perfect for chilly autumn days. The lamb needs to be tender – boned leg is ideal. Serve with saffron rice, Spätzli (see recipe p152) or Rösti (see recipe p155).

Method

1. Heat half the butter and the oil together over a high heat in a large, heavy-based frying pan. Add a handful of cubed lamb and fry quickly until browned – take care not to overcook. Remove from the pan and transfer to a bowl. Repeat this process until all the meat has been browned. Sprinkle with salt and freshly ground black pepper and keep warm.

2. Reduce the heat and add the remaining butter together with the onion and the garlic. Cook gently until they have softened but not browned. Add the chilli, tomatoes, lemon zest and juice, stock and sugar, stirring well to incorporate the juices left by the meat on the bottom of the pan. Return the lamb to the pan and bring to a simmer over a low heat for 1½ - 2 hours, until the meat is tender.

3. To make the beurre manié place the soft butter and flour together in a small bowl and blend together. Set aside.

4. Meanwhile make the saffron rice. Place all the ingredients together in a heavy-based saucepan. Bring to the boil then reduce the heat until the rice is just simmering. Cover with a close-fitting lid and cook for 20 minutes. Remove from the heat and leave to stand for 10 minutes, then fluff up with a fork before serving.

5. Remove the lamb from the heat and stir in the prepared beurre manié together with the drained chickpeas. Return to a low heat and cook for a further 5 minutes to thicken the sauce. Before serving, sprinkle with the fresh coriander.

Ingredients

Serves 5 - 6

50g butter

1 teaspoon olive oil

1kg lean lamb, cut into cubes approximately 2cm in size

salt & freshly ground black pepper

1 medium onion, finely chopped

2 garlic cloves, crushed

1 small red chilli, very finely chopped

4 large plum tomatoes, skin removed and chopped, or one 400g tin

grated zest and juice of 1 lemon

200ml vegetable stock (recipe p237) or vegetable bouillon

2 teaspoons sugar

250g cooked chickpeas, or one 400g tin, drained

1 tablespoon fresh coriander, chopped

For the beurre manié

30g soft butter

15g plain white flour

For the saffron rice

570ml water

400g basmati rice

¾ teaspoon salt

10g butter

2 or 3 pinches of saffron strands

Zürigeschnetzeltes
(Veal & Mushrooms in Cream Sauce)

This traditional Swiss recipe is said to have been developed by Herr Direktor Hammer, who ran the famous Bellevoir hotel school in Zürich. Translated the name means 'sliced meat from Zürich'. The ingredients are simple and readily available in Switzerland – the end result is a dish of true sophistication.

The cut of veal needs to be tender – topside is ideal. The mushrooms should be small – wild or button varieties are best. Serve with Rösti (see recipe p155), or Spätzli (see recipe p152) and a crisp green salad.

Method

1. Put half the butter, together with the olive oil, into a heavy-based frying or sauteuse pan. Place over a high heat. Add a handful of the sliced veal and fry quickly until browned – do not overcook at this stage. Remove the veal and transfer to a bowl. Repeat this process until all the meat has been browned. Sprinkle with salt and freshly ground black pepper and keep warm.

2. Reduce the heat and add the remaining butter together with the onion. Cook gently until softened but not browned. Add the mushrooms and lemon juice. Cook over a moderate heat, stirring occasionally until the juice from the mushrooms has evaporated.

3. Next add the wine, keeping the pan over a moderate heat, and continue to cook until the juices have reduced by three quarters. Then add the cream and simmer until the sauce has thickened so that it will coat the back of a wooden spoon without running off immediately – 'coating consistency'.

4. Return the veal to the pan. Keep over a moderate heat for a few seconds and stir well to coat the meat with the sauce. Check the seasoning and adjust if necessary. Sprinkle with parsley and serve immediately.

Ingredients

Serves 4 - 5

50g butter

1 teaspoon olive oil

800g tender boneless veal, sliced into very thin strips

salt & freshly ground black pepper

1 medium onion, finely chopped

250g button or small wild mushrooms, finely sliced

3 teaspoons freshly squeezed lemon juice

200ml dry white wine

200ml double cream

1 tablespoon fresh parsley, chopped

Ingredients

Serves 4 – 6

300g plain white flour

1 teaspoon salt

3 medium eggs

200ml semi-skimmed milk

large knob of butter

freshly ground black pepper

Spätzli
(Miniature Swiss Dumplings)

Translated literally, spätzli is a Swiss-German word meaning 'little sparrows'. They are tiny Swiss dumplings, irregular in shape, made from a thick batter which is extruded through a special sieve and dropped into gently boiling water. They can be served with butter or grated cheese as an accompaniment to meat, or with any sauce suitable for pasta. My father-in-law, Victor, always makes a huge batch to be eaten with the turkey on Christmas Day.

If you do not have a spätzli sieve, make a slightly stiffer batter by reducing the liquid content. Spread it onto a wooden board and slice it into tiny pieces with a sharp knife. Make sure you use cold water to clean any equipment that will come into contact with the batter; hot water will cook it, welding it firmly to any surface it has touched.

Spätzli keep very well in the freezer for up to 2 months.

Method

1. Using a wooden spoon, mix the flour and salt together in a large bowl, then make a well in the centre.

2. Whisk the eggs and milk together in a jug and add to the well in the centre of the flour bit by bit. Using a wooden spoon gradually draw the flour into the liquid before adding more, until a thick batter has formed. The amount of liquid required may vary depending on the size of the eggs and the moisture content of the flour. To check for the correct consistency, lift a spoonful of batter above the bowl – it should break off the spoon and fall back into the bowl – this is known as 'snapping' consistency.

3. Once the correct texture has been achieved, beat the batter briskly with a wooden spoon for a minute or two. This is to incorporate air and develop the gluten, giving the batter elasticity.

4. Cover with cling film and leave in the bowl for a minimum of 30 minutes to rest – after which the batter should be silky in texture and air bubbles should be rising to the surface.

5. Being well organised at this stage really pays off. Choose a large, heavy-based pan onto which the spätzli sieve fits snugly. Half fill it with salted water and bring to a rolling boil. Place a clean plate large enough to hold the sieve next to the pan of water and leave the sieve on it whenever it is not in use – it is important to minimise the time the sieve is actually over the pan of water. This is to keep it cool and avoid cooking the batter before it has been completely extruded. On the other side of the pan, have a large baking tray dotted with butter ready to take the hot spätzli. You will also need a large slotted spoon or small sieve to scoop the spätzli out of the boiling water, and a scraper to push the batter through the sieve.

6. Resting the spätzli sieve on the clean plate, spoon a small dollop of batter into the centre – do not be tempted to use too much at once. Place the sieve over the top of the pan and quickly press the batter through the holes with the scraper. Remove the sieve as soon as all the batter has been pushed through, and return it to the plate. The spätzli will float to the top of the pan when they are ready. Remove them with the slotted spoon and spread them on the buttered baking tray to cool. Repeat this process until all the batter has been used. The spätzli can be frozen at this point.

7. To serve, place a large knob of butter in a heavy-based non-stick frying pan and add the spätzli. Sprinkle with a little freshly ground black pepper and fry until golden.

Rösti

Rösti is a delicious fried potato cake from Switzerland. Originally from the Swiss-German speaking area around Bern, it is now served throughout the country, often as an accompaniment to meat. However, I believe some of the best Röstis are those which are tasty enough to be a main course dish in themselves. In this recipe the grated potato is enriched with cream, finely chopped onion and cheese – from this base any number of additional ingredients can be added. Experiment with cooked bacon lardons, slivers of smoked salmon, grated parsnip, courgettes or carrots, shredded savoy cabbage or chopped herbs.

Swiss cheese is a very appropriate topping – try Gruyère, raclette, Emmental or appenzeller, browned under the grill.

Perfect Rösti is very simple to make, provided you follow a few simple rules:-

- start the day before you wish to serve the Rösti.

- use a good waxy potato such us 'Wilja' or 'Estima'. I have also used 'Charlottes' from our garden which work well.

- the potatoes must be partially cooked through but not too well done. The amount of time they require will depend on their size. To check whether they are ready slice one in half – the flesh should change colour about a third of the way through towards the centre.

- don't be tempted to speed up the cooling process of the potatoes by rinsing them under cold water or putting them in the fridge – they must be left at room temperature for at least 3 or 4 hours (preferably overnight) to cool naturally. This enables the retained heat in the potato to cook the centre a little more.

- make sure you grate the potato coarsely – if grated too finely the strands of cooked potato will amalgamate together when fried and not remain distinct.

Ingredients

Makes 2 individual Röstis, 15cm in diameter, or one large Rösti 24cm in diameter, or 4 baby Röstis 7cm in diameter

500g waxy potatoes ('Wilja', 'Estima' or 'Charlotte')

25g butter

1 small onion, finely chopped

75g Gruyère cheese, finely grated

75ml whipping cream

½ teaspoon salt

freshly ground black pepper

Rösti

- use a good, heavy-based non-stick frying pan.

- fry the Rösti gently so that a golden brown crust forms on the outside. If fried too quickly the inside will be raw.

Method

1. Wash the potatoes thoroughly, do not peel. Bring a large, heavy-based pan of salted water to the boil, then add the potatoes. Bring back to the boil and simmer gently for 10 - 15 minutes, depending on the size of the potatoes. To test, a sharp knife should penetrate the flesh without too much resistance, but they should not be cooked through. Transfer the potatoes to a colander and allow to cool naturally at room temperature for at least 3 - 4 hours, preferably overnight.

2. When completely cold, peel the potatoes carefully, then grate them coarsely using a hand grater. Place them in a large bowl and set aside.

3. In a heavy-based frying pan, soften the onions in the butter until translucent. Allow to cool slightly, then add to the grated potato in the bowl. Next add the Gruyère cheese, whipping cream, salt and freshly ground black pepper, mixing all the ingredients together thoroughly.

4. Place a heavy-based non-stick frying pan over a moderate heat for a few moments before adding the Rösti mixture. Press it well down to form a potato cake. Fry gently for approximately 6 - 8 minutes until the underside is crusty and golden. To turn, take a plate the same size as the Rösti and place it upside down on the uncooked surface. Turn the plate and pan upside down together so that the Rösti is now on the plate. Slide the Rösti back into the pan and cook the other side for approximately 6 - 8 minutes. When golden on both sides, serve immediately or cover with a topping and grill if necessary. Delicious with Zürigeschnetzeltes (see recipe p151), Lamb & Chickpea Stew (see recipe p149), and Mushrooms in Wine & Cream (see recipe p129).

Tarte Tatin

This 'upside down' apple tart is a speciality of the Sologne District in the Loire Valley of France. The 'Demoiselles Tatin' were two impoverished gentlewomen who, in straitened circumstances, were forced to earn their living by baking and selling their father's favourite dessert.

Although this dish looks and tastes spectacular, it is really very simple to make. Many of the recipes I have tried have been unsuccessful, usually resulting in rather soggy pastry swimming in liquid. The trick, I have discovered through experience, is to cook the apples slowly over a low to medium heat in the butter and sugar mixture until the juice from the apples has evaporated and the fruit has become dark and caramelised.

It is essential to use dessert apples – cooking apples will 'fall' and become mushy.

The recipe for the pastry is on p230, but if you prefer you can use shop-bought which works very well.

Method

1. Roll out the puff pastry on a lightly floured surface until it is slightly larger than a 24cm heavy-based ovenproof frying pan or skillet, and roughly 5mm thick.

2. Turn the pan upside down and make an impression on the pastry with the rim. Using this as a guide, cut a circle out of the pastry, 1 cm larger than the pan all round. Cover the circle of pastry in cling film and set aside in the fridge until required.

3. Peel, core and halve the apples. If you are preparing them in advance, keep them in a bowl of cold water to prevent discolouration.

4. Over a low heat melt the butter in the pan and add the sugar, stirring until it has dissolved. Do not allow the mixture to colour at all at this stage.

Ingredients

Serves 8

500g puff pastry (recipe p230)

13 or 14 small to medium dessert apples

125g butter

200g caster sugar

APPLES

We grow 'Cox's Orange Pippins' in our garden which are delicious in Tarte Tatin. They have a crisp, juicy, firm texture with a sweet flavour, balanced by a little acidity. The better the flavour of the apples, the tastier the tart will be.

Tarte Tatin

5. Next, arrange the halved apples around the pan, standing them on their ends, forming an interlocking circle of fruit. You should have room for a second circle of apples in the centre.

6. Place on a moderate heat making sure all of the butter and sugar mixture is bubbling gently. The juice will come out of the fruit and gradually evaporate. After a while, the apples will start to colour as the butter and sugar begins to caramelise. This can take up to 45 minutes – don't be tempted to speed up the process. Preheat the oven to 190°C (gas mark 5).

7. When the apples are cooked and the caramel is a deep rich colour, remove from the heat and allow to cool for a few minutes.

8. Remove the pastry from the fridge and place over the apples, tucking it down inside the rim of the pan.

9. Place in the preheated oven for approximately 45 minutes, until the pastry is crisp, well risen and dark golden in colour. Remove from the oven and leave in the pan until required.

10. To turn out, briefly loosen the apples and caramel by warming the pan over a low heat. Place a serving plate upside down over the pan, then quickly turn the pan and plate over together. You will now have the pastry on the bottom and the apples on the top. Once turned out, the tart can be kept warm in a low oven. Best served warm with cream, crème fraîche or Vanilla Ice Cream (see recipe p105).

Lemon Soufflé Pudding

This recipe takes me straight back to childhood. From an early age, it was my job to make a pudding to follow the Sunday roast, and this was my favourite. When the mixture goes into the oven, it is sloppy and curdled – magically it emerges as a light, fluffy sponge with a delicious lemon curd sauce beneath.

You will need a baking dish approximately 24cm in diameter and 6cm deep, preferably made from porcelain, which is a very efficient conductor of heat – this helps the sauce to set at the bottom of the pudding. Alternatively, you could use individual soufflé dishes.

Method

1. Preheat the oven to 180°C (gas mark 4). Beat the butter and sugar together in a large mixing bowl until well amalgamated. Add the grated lemon zest and juice, followed by the flour, then gradually add the milk, whisking each ingredient in well. Finally, beat in the egg yolks.

2. In a clean bowl with clean beaters, whisk the egg whites until they form stiff peaks.

3. Using a metal spoon, gently fold the stiffly beaten egg whites into the butter and sugar mixture, one spoonful at a time, taking care not to knock the air out of the egg whites. Pour the mixture into the baking dish.

4. Stand the baking dish in a roasting tin and pour boiling water around it, to a depth of 3 or 4 cm – it is easier to do this once the roasting tin and pudding are standing in the oven. Bake in the preheated oven for 30 minutes, then turn the temperature down to 150°C (gas mark 2), and bake for a further 15 minutes. The top should be risen and browned and feel firm to the touch. Pierce with a skewer to check that the sauce has thickened. If it is still runny, turn the oven down to 100°C (gas mark ¼), and leave for a little longer. Serve with fresh pouring cream.

Ingredients

Serves 8

175g butter, at room temperature

400g caster sugar

grated zest and juice of 3 lemons

125g plain white flour

600ml semi-skimmed milk

3 medium eggs, separated

Apple Cake

This is a beautiful moist cake, which tastes even better the day after it is made. The thinly sliced apples are enveloped in a zesty lemon sponge sprinkled with almonds – a delicious combination of flavours. Make sure you use dessert apples – cooking apples will 'fall' and turn to mush in the oven.

Method

1. Line the sides and base of a 20cm diameter cake tin with baking parchment, using a little melted butter under the parchment to help it stay in place. Preheat the oven to 175°C (gas mark 3½).

2. In a large bowl, beat the butter and sugar together until creamy and light in colour. Add the egg yolks one by one followed by the lemon zest and juice. Combine the flour, baking powder and salt together and stir into the butter and egg yolk mixture.

3. In a separate bowl, whisk the egg whites until stiff, then add a small amount to the cake mixture and stir gently to slacken. Now fold in the remainder of the egg whites spoonful by spoonful, taking care not to knock air out of the mixture.

4. Peel, core and halve the apples. With the curved side uppermost, and without cutting completely through, make as many fine slices as possible lengthways in each half.

5. Spoon the mixture into the prepared cake tin, then push the sliced apple halves into the mixture curved side up, spacing them evenly. Sprinkle the surface with the almonds then bake in the preheated oven for approximately 30 – 40 minutes, until golden and firm. To check it is ready, pierce the centre of the cake with a thin skewer, avoiding the apples – it should come out clean.

6. When ready, allow to stand for a few minutes in the cake tin, then remove and leave to cool on a cooling rack.

Ingredients

Makes a 20cm diameter cake

- 125g butter, at room temperature
- 125g caster sugar
- 3 large eggs, separated
- grated zest of 1 lemon and juice of ½ lemon
- 125g plain white flour, sifted to remove any lumps
- 1 teaspoon baking powder
- pinch of salt
- 3 small, good-flavoured, firm dessert apples
- 2 tablespoons strip or flaked almonds

ALMONDS

Sweet almonds are the most widely cultivated of all the nut trees and are used the world over in both savoury and sweet dishes. The nut grows inside a hard, oval shell which must be removed before use. They have a mild flavour which adds richness and moisture to cakes and desserts.

Scones

These scones are light and buttery. For a change of flavour try adding chopped candied orange peel, lemon peel, and zest, diced apricots or dates, or for savoury scones substitute the sugar and sultanas with freshly grated Parmesan cheese and a little dry mustard powder. The mixture freezes very well uncooked.

Method

1. Preheat the oven to 220°C (gas mark 7). Line a large baking tray with baking parchment. Place the self raising flour and butter in a large bowl. Very gently begin to bring the flour and butter together by rubbing between your thumb and fingertips, allowing it to fall from a short height above the bowl. This will incorporate air into the scones making them beautifully light. Continue in this way until the mixture resembles fine breadcrumbs.

2. Add the salt, caster sugar, sultanas, lightly beaten eggs and sufficient milk to bring everything together to form a soft dough. The amount of milk will vary accordingly to the size of the eggs, softness of the butter and the temperature of the room. Avoid working the dough too much.

3. Turn the dough out onto a lightly floured work surface, flour a rolling pin well and roll the dough out until it is approximately 2cm thick. Cut it into squares or diamond shapes with a sharp knife and transfer to the prepared baking tray, making sure you leave space between them for expansion. Brush the tops with a little milk, then bake in the preheated oven for approximately 10 minutes. Serve warm with clotted cream or butter and home-made jam (see recipe p107).

Ingredients

Makes approximately 15

500g self raising flour, sieved to remove any lumps

175g soft butter, cut into very small pieces

pinch of salt

3 tablespoons caster sugar

150g sultanas

2 large eggs, lightly beaten

a little milk

Walnut Tart

This unusual old English recipe combines the flavour of treacle tart with the delicate sweetness of walnuts. It has a passing resemblance to American pecan pie, but I think this tart is superior in every way.

Method

1. First make the pastry as described on p232. Remove from the fridge and allow to almost reach room temperature. Lightly dust the work surface and rolling pin with flour and begin to roll out the pastry lightly but firmly. Keep turning it and dusting the work surface to prevent it from sticking and continue until the pastry is larger than your tart case and approximately 3mm thick. Roll it around the rolling pin and lift it onto the tart case. Gently coax it down the sides, making sure it isn't stretched. Trim off the excess with a sharp knife. Place in the fridge and leave to rest for at least 20 minutes.

2. Preheat the oven to 180°C (gas mark 4). When the pastry has rested, take a piece of baking parchment a little larger than the tart case, screw it into a ball, then flatten it out over the surface of the pastry. Cover the top with ceramic baking beans or rice. Bake in the preheated oven for 10 minutes, then remove the paper and beans and return to the oven for a further 10 minutes, until the pastry is golden. Remove and set aside to cool.

3. Meanwhile, make the filling. Place the butter and sugar in a large mixing bowl and beat together until pale and creamy. Next add the eggs one by one, followed by the golden syrup, lemon juice and zest. Finally, add the walnuts. The mixture will look rather curdled at this stage – don't worry.

4. Pour the filling into the prepared pastry case and place in the oven. Bake for 15 minutes at 180°C (gas mark 4), then lower the temperature to 150°C (gas mark 2), and bake for a further 25 minutes. This tart is delicious served hot or cold. Try it with Vanilla Ice Cream (see recipe p105).

Ingredients

For a 22cm fluted tart case
Serves 8

- 500g sweet pastry (recipe p232)
- 125g butter, at room temperature
- 125g soft brown sugar
- 3 medium eggs
- 190g golden syrup
- grated zest and juice of 1 lemon
- 250g shelled walnut pieces

WALNUTS

Brought to England by the Romans, who believed them to be the food of the gods, walnuts have always been valued for their sweet and delicate flavour. They are exceptionally rich in omega-3 polyunsaturated linolenic acid, which supports the immune and cardiovascular systems.

Plum Frangipane Tart

Fruit tarts made with frangipane are typical of the Normandy region of France. The frangipane base can be used with most fruits, apple being the most common, but pears, apricots, cherries and nectarines also work very well.

Method

1. First make the pastry as described on p232. Remove from the fridge and allow to almost reach room temperature. Dust the work surface and rolling pin with flour and begin to roll out the pastry lightly but firmly. Keep turning it and dusting the work surface to ensure it doesn't stick. The pastry needs to be larger than the tart case and approximately 3mm thick. Roll the pastry around the rolling pin and lift it onto the tart case. Gently coax it down the sides, making sure you don't stretch it. Trim off the excess with a sharp knife. Place in the fridge and leave to rest for at least 20 minutes.

2. Preheat the oven to 180°C (gas mark 4). When the pastry has rested, take a piece of baking parchment a little larger than the tart case, screw it into a ball, then flatten it out over the top of the pastry. Cover the surface with ceramic baking beans or rice. Bake in the oven for 10 minutes, then remove the paper and beans and return it to the oven for a further 10 minutes until the pastry is golden. Remove and set aside to cool.

3. Meanwhile make the frangipane. Place the butter and sugar in a bowl and cream together until the mixture is light and soft. Add the eggs one by one, beating well. Next add the Kirsch, then finally stir in the ground almonds and flour. Spoon into the tart case.

4. Arrange the halved plums on their sides in circles, starting at the edge of the tart and working your way towards the centre, pushing them well into the frangipane mixture.

Ingredients

For a 28cm fluted tart case
Serves 8 – 10

500g sweet pastry (recipe p232)

20 or so dessert plums, halved, with the stones removed

For the frangipane

135g butter

135g caster sugar

2 medium eggs, lightly beaten

2 teaspoons Kirsch

160g ground almonds

55g plain white flour

For the glaze

2 or 3 tablespoons apricot jam

1 tablespoon water

Plum Frangipane Tart

5. Place the tart in the preheated oven for approximately 45 - 50 minutes, until the frangipane is golden brown and set. Remove from the oven and set aside to cool.

6. To make the glaze, melt the apricot jam and water together in a small pan over a low heat – it should resemble thick syrup. When the tart is cool, brush the surface with the glaze. Serve at room temperature with pouring cream, crème fraîche or Vanilla Ice Cream (see recipe p105).

PLUMS

Plum trees are believed to have originated in China, where they symbolise good fortune. They are a rich source of calcium, magnesium, vitamin A, iron, potassium and dietary fibre. This sweet, juicy variety growing in our garden is 'Marjorie'. We also grow 'Victorias', which are ready a little earlier.

Crab Apple & Quince Jelly

This jelly is a perfect accompaniment for Loin of Pork with Parsley Stuffing (see recipe p145). Crab apples and quinces can be used in any proportion – whatever you can find in the garden or hedgerows. Its jewel-like colour is almost as beautiful as its fragrant flavour.

Method

1. Wash the crab apples and quinces well and remove any blemished parts. Cut them into quarters and put into a large, heavy-based pan. Add enough cold water so that it is level with the top of the fruit. Simmer until soft and pulpy. Leave to cool slightly then pour the pulp into a jelly bag suspended above a large bowl and leave overnight.

2. The following day, measure the juice that has strained through the jelly bag into the bowl. For every pint, allow 1lb sugar – 570ml of juice to 450g sugar.

3. Sterilise your jars and lids by preheating the oven to 180°C (gas mark 4). Wash the jars and lids in hot soapy water and then rinse – do not dry with a tea towel. Place them on a baking sheet and leave in the oven for at least 10 minutes. Remove and allow to cool slightly.

4. Place the juice and sugar into a heavy-based pan together with the lemon rind and juice. Bring to the boil slowly, stirring well to dissolve the sugar, then boil rapidly, skimming off any froth that forms. When the mixture has started to thicken and look like jelly (10 - 20 minutes), test for setting. Leave a plate in the fridge for a few minutes. Spoon a small quantity of jelly onto the cold plate – it will be at setting point if it wrinkles when pushed with your finger.

5. Leave to cool for 5 minutes, then pour the jelly into the sterilised jars. Either remove the lemon peel or place a piece in each jar for decoration. Cover with a waxed disc, wax side down, then seal with the lids whilst still hot. Allow to cool for 24 hours before labelling and storing in a cool dark place.

Ingredients

a good amount of mixed crab apples and quinces – up to 4kg

pared rind and juice of 2 lemons

granulated sugar

Sloe Gin

These hard, small fruits of the blackthorn tree are too bitter to eat, but by steeping them in gin for four or five months the reward is a rich burgundy-coloured liqueur. This recipe can also be used with damsons, the cultivated cousins of the sloe. It will make quite a 'dry' sloe gin. If you prefer something a little sweeter, increase the amount of sugar.

Method

1. Wash the sloes thoroughly and discard any soft or damaged fruit.

2. Prick each one with a pointed knife. Alternatively place them in a freezer for a day or two until they are frozen and the skins start to burst open, then defrost.

3. Sterilise a large glass jar by preheating the oven to 180°C (gas mark 4). Wash the jar and lid in soapy water, rinse, then place on a baking sheet and leave in the oven for at least 10 minutes. Remove and allow to cool.

4. Place the sloes in the jar, then add the sugar and gin.

5. Shake the jar daily for the first three or four weeks then store in a cool place for a further three months, shaking occasionally.

6. After four months, pour the sloe gin through a strainer lined with moistened muslin and decant into bottles. It still needs to mature so don't be tempted to try it too soon. Some people are happy to drink it after six months, others say it is better at the ten-month stage.

Ingredients

Makes approximately 1 litre

approximately 1kg sloes

200g caster sugar

1 litre gin

SLOES

Sloes are the fruit of the blackthorn tree, commonly found in country hedgerows. In autumn, sloe bushes can be recognised by their long sharp thorns and small, hard blue-black skinned fruit, reminiscent of miniature damsons. They are 'wild food' and can be gathered by anyone with thick gloves and perseverance.

Winter

Recipes

Swiss Pearl Barley Soup

This robust and nutritious winter soup comes from the Graubünden, an area in the south-eastern Alps of Switzerland. It is a delicious combination of seasonal root vegetables, pearl barley and small pieces of air-dried beef or ham, enriched with cream and egg yolks. If you make it in advance, do not add the cream and egg yolks until after you have re-heated it – if they boil, the eggs will coagulate and become lumpy.

Method

1. In a large, heavy-based pan, soften the onions, leeks, carrots and celeriac in the butter, without allowing them to colour. Add the pearl barley and meat and cook for a further 2 - 3 minutes, stirring well.

2. Mix in the flour, then add the stock gradually whilst continuing to stir. Season with the salt and freshly ground black pepper, then bring to the boil and simmer gently for 1 - 1½ hours, until the pearl barley is cooked through. Remove the pan from the heat.

3. To finish, reheat the soup, then mix the lightly beaten egg yolks and cream together and stir into the soup. Check the seasoning and sprinkle with the chives. Serve with fresh, crusty bread such as Swiss Fitness Loaf (see recipe p179), or Pumpkin-seed Bread (see recipe p123).

Ingredients

Serves 8

25g butter

2 onions, finely diced

2 small leeks, finely diced

3 carrots, finely diced

50g celeriac, finely diced

150g pearl barley

150g air-dried beef or ham, finely chopped

2 tablespoons plain white flour

2 litres vegetable stock (recipe p237) or vegetable bouillon

salt & freshly ground black pepper

2 egg yolks, lightly beaten

250ml whipping cream

fresh chives, chopped

Swiss Fitness Loaf

This wholesome bread is full of good things. It has a moist, dense texture packed with seeds which give it a delicious nutty flavour.

I love this bread with wild smoked salmon.

Method

1. Place the flour, seeds, salt and butter in a large mixing bowl. Rub the butter into the flour until the mixture resembles fine breadcrumbs.

2. In a small jug, dissolve the yeast in the tepid water, then stir in the honey.

3. Make a well in the centre of the dry ingredients and pour in the yeast mixture. Mix together by hand until a soft dough has formed.

4. Remove the dough from the bowl and knead on a lightly floured surface for approximately 10 minutes. This is quite a sticky dough, so try and keep it moving, dusting the work surface with more flour as necessary. When the dough has become smooth and elastic, divide it into 2 equal portions and mould into balls. Leave them to rest for 5 minutes then shape into loaves and place in lightly greased small loaf tins.

5. Cover the loaves with cling film and leave in a warm place to prove for approximately 1½ hours. They will be ready when they have doubled in size and the dough springs back slowly when pressed. Preheat the oven to 200°C (gas mark 6).

6. Bake in the preheated oven for 25 - 30 minutes until golden on top. To test if they are ready, tap the base of the loaves – they should sound hollow.

Ingredients

Makes 2 loaves

- 450g stoneground wholemeal flour
- 40g sunflower seeds
- 40g linseeds
- 40g poppy seeds
- 1½ teaspoons salt
- 15g butter
- 20g fresh yeast (or 10g dried yeast)
- 300ml tepid water
- 1 tablespoon honey

SEEDS

Seeds are made up of two parts – an embryonic shoot surrounded by tissue which is designed as a food supply to fuel its initial growth. This outer layer contains hundreds of chemicals which help to protect our bodies against cancer, heart disease and diabetes. Linseeds are a rich source of omega-3 fatty acids, whilst sunflower seeds contain high levels of antioxidants and vitamin E.

Smoked Salmon & Prawn Parcels

Delicious as a starter or light lunch, the combination of smoked salmon, prawns and mayonnaise in this recipe is delicate and refreshing. Wild smoked salmon is the best; Atlantic or Pacific is quite readily available these days. Use the smallest cold-water prawns you can find – avoid the large warm-water varieties which have a rather rubbery texture.

Method

1. Place the prawns, mayonnaise and chives together in a small bowl, add a sprinkling of black pepper, and carefully mix together.

2. Neatly line six small ramekins (roughly 7cm wide and 3½cm deep) with the slices of smoked salmon, leaving several centimetres hanging over the sides.

3. Spoon the prawn mixture into the lined ramekins, then fold the edges of the smoked salmon into the centre to form the parcels. Press down firmly and chill in the fridge for several hours.

4. To serve, turn each ramekin upside down onto a plate and shake. The parcel should fall out easily, but can be released with a small knife if necessary. Lay a sprig of fresh dill on the top of each parcel and garnish with a lemon wedge and fresh salad leaves. Delicious with Swiss Fitness Loaf (see recipe p179).

Ingredients

Makes 6

350g small prawns

6 tablespoons fresh mayonnaise (recipe p239)

5 teaspoons fresh chives, finely chopped

freshly ground black pepper

300g smoked salmon, sliced

6 sprigs of fresh dill

6 lemon wedges

Potted Cheese

This is the ideal way to use up the remains of a large piece of cheese. It keeps very well in the fridge covered with a layer of melted butter. Serve it either as a starter or at the end of a meal in place of a cheeseboard. Most hard English cheeses can be used – but being from Yorkshire, white or blue Wensleydale is my personal preference.

Method

1. Place the grated cheese in a large mixing bowl. Add the butter and mix together to form a paste.

2. When well amalgamated, work in the port and cayenne pepper.

3. Transfer to one large pot or individual ramekins and place in the fridge to set. If you wish, you can decorate the surface with walnuts or flat-leaved parsley. Serve with crusty bread or oatcakes.

Ingredients

Serves 6

250g hard cheese such as white or blue Wensleydale, Stilton, Cheshire, Swaledale, single Gloucester or Coverdale, finely grated

85g butter, at room temperature

2 – 3 tablespoons port

pinch of cayenne pepper

walnuts and flat-leaved parsley for decoration

WENSLEYDALE CHEESE

In Yorkshire, traditionally, fruit cake is served with a piece of Wensleydale cheese, hence the saying 'a piece of cake without some cheese is like a kiss without a squeeze'. Wensleydale is still made in the market town of Hawes, in the original creamery. It has a delicate flavour and slightly crumbly texture. Blue Wensleydale, with its fine veining and superb taste, is more than a match for any Stilton.

Grilled Raclette

Raclette cheese is a speciality of the Valais, the south-west region of Switzerland bordering Italy and France. The landscape varies from majestic mountains such as the Matterhorn, to the flat-bottomed valley of the Rhône river. The steep slopes above the Rhône are carpeted with vineyards in which many unusual grape varieties grow, some dating back to Roman times. Standing in a sunny vineyard above Sion, gazing at the splendid mountain panorama whilst sipping a glass of Heida or Arvine is a rare treat.

The farmers whose cattle graze the high Alps of the Valais in the summer produce their own cheese, hence the raclette from one valley can be very different in flavour from that of a neighbouring valley.

The Château de Villa restaurant in Sierre, where I have enjoyed raclette many times with André Darbellay, our Swiss wine producer, serves four or five different cheeses in succession, saving the most pungent until the last. The wine served with a raclette meal is always white – traditionally a local Fendant.

The best raclettes are made from unpasteurised milk and are aged for at least 6 months. The original way of melting raclette was to hold the cut surface of half a wheel of cheese close to the embers of an open fire. As it melted, it was scraped off, an action which gives it its name, 'racler', meaning 'to scrape' in French. Nowadays, there are easier ways of melting the cheese. The ingenious Swiss have developed a range of electric table-top devices to do the job – but the simplest method is to lay several slices of raclette complete with rind, in the bottom of an ovenproof skillet and place it under a hot grill. Serve with baby pickled gherkins, silverskin onions and small boiled potatoes. Delicious with Lamb's Lettuce Salad with Swiss Dressing (see recipe p187).

Ingredients

Per person

- 125g Swiss raclette cheese
- 80g small potatoes, scrubbed well

To garnish

- small gherkins or cornichons
- cocktail-sized silverskin onions

Grilled Raclette

Method

1. Turn on the grill to its maximum setting. Cook the well-scrubbed potatoes in salted boiling water until they pierce easily with a small sharp knife. Drain and keep warm, wrapped in a clean tea towel inside a basket or serving dish.

2. Cut the raclette into slices approximately 4 - 5mm thick, leaving the rind in place. Lay the slices in the bottom of individual ovenproof skillets and place under the hot grill. The cheese will be ready to eat when it has melted and started to bubble. Finally, garnish with the onions and gherkins. To be authentic, serve with Swiss Fendant.

SWISS WINE

From the Bonvin vineyards above Sion the views take in the Rhône Valley with the Alps in the distance. The mountainsides are steeply terraced requiring much of the hand-picked grape harvest to be collected by helicopter. Several ancient grape varieties are still grown here, believed to have been brought to the region by the Romans.

Lamb's Lettuce Salad with Swiss Dressing

Lamb's lettuce (known as 'mâche' or 'nüsslisalat' in Switzerland) is one of the few salad ingredients that can be grown successfully outdoors throughout the winter. It survives both severe frosts and heavy snowfall, as we know from experience in our own vegetable garden in Yorkshire.

The Swiss salad dressing contains cream which gives it a smooth luxurious texture. It will keep for 3 – 4 days in the fridge.

Method

1. Place all the ingredients for the dressing together in a jug or small bowl. Blend together with a small whisk until creamy and emulsified. The dressing should not be too thick – if necessary, a little water can be added to give a light coating consistency.

2. Place the lamb's lettuce in a large salad bowl. Sprinkle with the chives. Drizzle with 2 – 3 tablespoons of the prepared dressing, toss lightly, then scatter the hardboiled egg on top of the leaves. Serve immediately.

Ingredients

Serves 5 – 6

180g lamb's lettuce

3 teaspoons fresh chives, finely chopped

1 medium egg, hardboiled and finely chopped

For the Swiss dressing

150ml extra virgin olive oil

150ml grape seed oil

100ml white wine vinegar

1 teaspoon smooth mustard

1 teaspoon caster sugar

2 tablespoons whipping cream

salt & freshly ground black pepper

LAMB'S LETTUCE

This hardy salad vegetable survives sub-zero temperatures as this photograph, taken in our garden in the middle of winter, demonstrates.

Puy Lentils with Rosemary & Chilli

Braised lentils are a wonderful accompaniment for roasted meat, and also make a delicious, protein-packed main course for vegetarians. They are an excellent source of cholesterol-lowering fibre.

I love the combination of flavours in this recipe – the rosemary with its slightly spicy aroma blends perfectly with the chilli. This dish keeps very well in the freezer for several months.

Method

1. Heat 1 tablespoon of the olive oil in a medium-sized, heavy-based saucepan and add the onion and garlic. Cook over a low heat until they have softened and become translucent but not coloured.

2. Next, add the rosemary, chilli and lentils. Cook for a further minute, then add the stock or vegetable bouillon. Bring to the boil, cover with a lid and simmer gently for 1 hour – most of the liquid should have been absorbed.

3. Before serving, add salt and freshly ground black pepper to taste. Finally, stir in the remaining olive oil followed by the red wine vinegar.

Ingredients

Serves 5 - 6

- 3 tablespoons extra virgin olive oil
- 1 medium red onion, finely chopped
- 2 garlic cloves, finely chopped
- 3 tablespoons fresh rosemary, finely chopped
- 1 small red chilli, very finely chopped
- 340g puy lentils, well rinsed
- 850ml vegetable stock (recipe p237) or vegetable bouillon
- salt & freshly ground black pepper
- ½ tablespoon red wine vinegar

CHILLIES

Chillies contain high levels of vitamins C and A and also have antibacterial properties. The smaller the chilli, the hotter it will be. This variety, grown in our greenhouse, is 'Ring-o-fire'.

Roast Fillet of Beef with Creamy Tomato Sauce

Fillet of beef is a special treat. Although it is one of the most expensive cuts of beef, it has no waste, so a little goes a long way. Serve it pink or rare to ensure it remains moist and succulent.

In this recipe, the juices from the meat blend with roasted tomatoes and garlic which are then combined with cream to make a mouth-watering sauce.

Method

1. Preheat the oven to 220°C (gas mark 7). Rub the surface of the meat with a little olive oil, then sprinkle with salt and freshly ground black pepper. Heat a little more oil in a large frying pan, add the meat and brown on all sides, then remove and keep warm.

2. Next, skin the tomatoes. The easiest way to do this is to cover them in boiling water for a few minutes until the skins split; they will then peel away easily. Cut the peeled tomatoes into halves, removing and discarding as many of the seeds as possible. Set aside.

3. Lay the browned fillet on a rack in a large roasting tin. Place the prepared tomatoes and garlic cloves, together with the water, under the meat in the bottom of the tin. Sprinkle with a little more salt and freshly ground black pepper. Place in the preheated oven. Allow 15 minutes per 450g of meat if you wish to serve it rare, or 20 minutes for medium. When roasted to your satisfaction, lift the meat off the rack, place on a warmed serving dish and leave to rest, covered with foil, while you prepare the sauce.

4. Scrape the tomato mixture and meat juices from the bottom of the roasting tin and transfer them to a heavy-based saucepan. Place over a moderate heat for a couple of minutes, stirring well. Add the cream and cook for a further 3 - 4 minutes.

Ingredients

Serves 8 - 10

- 1.5kg piece of beef fillet, well trimmed
- extra virgin olive oil
- salt & freshly ground black pepper
- 12 - 15 large fresh plum tomatoes
- 3 garlic cloves, peeled and left whole
- 3 tablespoons water
- 150ml double cream

SPROUTS

Sprouts, if harvested when young and small and cooked until just tender (4 - 5 minutes), are one of the most delicious winter vegetables. They are full of vitamin C and A, fibre, iron, phosphorus and potassium.

Roast Fillet of Beef with Creamy Tomato Sauce

Ingredients

Serves 6 – 8

100g butter, at room temperature

900g waxy potatoes, peeled and very finely sliced

450g celeriac, peeled and finely sliced

salt & freshly ground black pepper

freshly grated nutmeg

450ml whole milk

450ml double cream

3 garlic cloves, crushed

5. Remove from the heat and blitz with a hand blender or pass through a sieve. You should have a smooth, creamy sauce. If it is a little too runny, return it to the heat and reduce it further until you have achieved a coating consistency. Check the seasoning and pour into a heated sauceboat. Delicious served with Potato & Celeriac Dauphinoise (see recipe below), Roasted Carrots & Beetroot (see recipe p205) and a crisp green seasonal vegetable such as sprouts or Savoy Cabbage (see p205).

Potato & Celeriac Dauphinoise

This is an interesting twist on a classic recipe. Use a waxy potato variety such as 'Estima', 'Wilja' or 'Charlotte', or a multi-purpose potato such as 'Desirée'. A mandolin will slice the potatoes very finely. This dish can be cooked in advance and reheated when required. Delicious with any roasted meat.

Method

1. Preheat the oven to 175°C (gas mark 3½). Brush the inside of a large ovenproof dish with a little of the butter. Begin to layer the potato and celeriac alternately in the dish, seasoning each layer with salt, pepper and a little nutmeg. Continue this process until all the potato and celeriac is used and the dish is full, finishing with a layer of potato.

2. Bring the milk, cream and garlic to the boil in a small, heavy-based saucepan. Pour over the layered potato and celeriac, then dot the surface with the remaining butter.

3. Place in the preheated oven and bake for approximately 1 hour, until the vegetables are tender and browned on top.

Lamb Shanks in Red Wine with Flageolet Beans

From the earliest of civilisations, beans have been dried to preserve them for use through the winter months. This is a hearty cold-weather dish which combines tender flageolet beans with succulent lamb braised in red wine.

If you don't have flageolet beans in your cupboard, haricot beans will do just as well. Dried beans should be soaked overnight before cooking. However, if you are short of time, cover them with a generous quantity of water, bring to the boil and leave to cool in the water for 40 minutes before continuing to cook according to the packet instructions. Drain well before proceeding with the recipe. Always add salt to beans at the end of the cooking time rather than at the beginning – adding it earlier will make them harden. Tinned beans are a perfectly acceptable alternative.

Method

1. Season the lamb shanks with salt and freshly ground black pepper. Pour several tablespoons of olive oil into a large, heavy-based frying pan. Place over a moderate heat, add the seasoned lamb and brown on all sides. Set aside.

2. Pour a little more olive oil into a heavy-based sauteuse pan or casserole and place over a moderate heat. Add the onions and garlic and cook for about 5 minutes until softened, stirring well. Add the red wine and boil for approximately 1 minute, then add the stock and soft brown sugar.

3. Next add the browned lamb shanks, followed by the thyme, rosemary and bay leaves. Bring to a simmer, cover with a lid and continue to cook gently for approximately 1½ - 2 hours, until the lamb is tender and coming away from the bone. Take care not to let it boil rapidly as this will toughen the meat.

Ingredients

Serves 4

4 small lamb shanks, 375 - 400g each

salt & freshly ground black pepper

extra virgin olive oil

2 medium onions, sliced

4 garlic cloves, peeled and left whole

500ml red wine

1 litre lamb stock (recipe p236) or bouillon

2 tablespoons soft light-brown sugar

2 sprigs of fresh thyme

2 sprigs of fresh rosemary

2 bay leaves

500g precooked flageolet beans (or 2 x 400g tins, drained)

For the beurre manié

30g soft butter

15g plain white flour

Lamb Shanks in Red Wine with Flageolet Beans

Ingredients

Serves 4

675g floury potatoes, peeled

salt & freshly ground black pepper

125ml milk

55g butter

a scraping of freshly grated nutmeg

4. Prepare the beurre manié by blending the butter and flour together in a small bowl. Set aside until required.

5. When the lamb is beautifully tender, remove the shanks from the pan and keep warm. Strain the cooking liquid into a clean pan, discarding the onions, garlic and herbs. Bring the liquid to the boil and reduce by two thirds. Stir in the prepared beurre manié and continue to cook for a further 5 minutes – this should thicken the liquid to a good coating consistency. Check the seasoning and adjust if necessary. Finally, add the flageolet beans and cook for a further minute.

6. Lay the lamb shanks in a deep serving dish, then add the sauce and beans. Serve with Buttery Mashed Potato (see recipe below).

Buttery Mashed Potato

This recipe will produce mash with a soft, creamy texture – if you prefer it a little stiffer, cut down the quantity of milk. Use a floury potato such as 'Golden Wonder' or an all purpose variety, for example 'Desirée'. To make delicious celeriac mash, substitute half the potatoes with diced celeriac.

Method

1. Place the potatoes in a large, heavy-based saucepan, cover with cold water, add a little salt and bring to the boil over a moderate heat. Allow to simmer for 15 - 20 minutes, until tender when pierced with a small knife.

2. When cooked, pour off the hot water and break up the potatoes with a masher. Add the black pepper, milk, butter and nutmeg and continue to mash until smooth.

Roast Goose with Apple, Pork & Walnut Stuffing

The tradition of serving goose at times of festivity and celebration goes back many centuries and is currently enjoying a revival. Geese tend to be reared naturally, grazing on pasture and stubble; they therefore have a limited season between September and January, making them the perfect choice for Christmas dinner. The meat is rich and succulent in texture with an intense flavour. The fat which naturally drains from the bird whilst it is roasting is highly valued and can be used to roast potatoes or parsnips, giving them extra crispness and flavour.

To carve the breast of the goose, first cut down one side of the breastbone, then cut the flesh into long wedges, working towards the leg.

Roasting time – allow 15 minutes per 450g plus an extra 20 minutes.

Method

1. First make the stuffing. Melt the butter in a large, heavy-based frying pan. Add the onions, apples, garlic, and minced pork and cook over a gentle heat, stirring occasionally, for about 15 minutes. Leave to cool slightly.

2. Place the breadcrumbs, walnuts, honey, eggs and parsley in a large bowl. Next, add the onion, apple and pork mixture, and season well. Combine together thoroughly and set aside until needed. Preheat the oven to 200°C (gas mark 6), and work out the cooking time required according to the guidelines above.

3. Remove the giblets from the cavity of the goose and set aside. Pluck any remaining quills from the skin with a pair of tweezers. Dry the inside of the bird with kitchen paper, then fill with the stuffing. Close the body cavity using a skewer to secure the skin.

Ingredients

Serves 6 – 8

- 1 free-range goose, approximately 4 - 4½kg in weight, with giblets
- salt & freshly ground black pepper

For the stuffing

- 100g butter
- 2 medium onions, finely chopped
- 4 large eating apples, peeled, cored and diced
- 2 large garlic cloves, crushed
- 700g minced pork
- 250g breadcrumbs
- 100g chopped walnuts
- 2 dessertspoons honey
- 2 large eggs, lightly beaten
- 2 tablespoons fresh parsley, chopped
- salt & freshly ground black pepper

For the beurre manié

- 30g soft butter
- 15g plain white flour

Roast Goose with Apple, Pork & Walnut Stuffing

4. Prick the skin of the goose all over with a sharp fork, then rub it liberally with salt and sprinkle with freshly ground black pepper. During roasting the fat will escape through the small holes you have made, and the salt will make the skin deliciously crispy.

5. Place the goose on a trivet or rack in a large roasting tin, breast side up. Wrap the legs in foil to prevent them from burning. Cover the rest of the bird with a loose layer of foil and place in the preheated oven. After the first hour, baste the goose with the fat from the bottom of the roasting tin. Pour off any surplus fat into a container. This can be used for roasting potatoes or parsnips.

6. While the goose is roasting, start the gravy. Place the giblets in approximately 2 litres of water in a heavy-based saucepan with a lid. Bring to the boil, then simmer gently over a low heat for approximately 1 hour. Strain and set aside.

7. Make the beurre manié by blending the soft butter and flour together in a small bowl, and set aside.

8. For the last half of roasting, remove the foil and discard, then baste the breast of the goose again, pouring off the surplus fat. When the breast is browned and crispy and the goose is cooked, lift it carefully onto a carving dish and leave to rest for approximately 20 minutes before serving.

9. To finish the gravy, pour any remaining fat out of the roasting tin then pour in the giblet liquor. Place over a low heat and stir well to incorporate the meat juices from the bottom of the roasting tin. Thicken with the prepared beurre manié.

Delicious with Casseroled Red Cabbage (see recipe p204), Roasted Parsnips (see recipe p202), Orange-glazed Carrots (see recipe p203), sprouts, Potato & Celeriac Dauphinoise (see recipe p192), and Crab Apple & Quince Jelly (see recipe p171).

Chestnut & Mushroom Roulade

The subtle flavours of the mushrooms, chestnuts and brazil nuts in the filling of this roulade complement each other perfectly. Although the plaiting of the pastry looks impressive and complicated, it is quite simple to do. Use a good quality all butter puff pastry, either shop-bought or home-made (see recipe p230) and precooked chestnuts – normally available in a vacuum pack from good supermarkets or delicatessens. Alternatively, if you know of the whereabouts of a sweet chestnut tree, you could prepare your own. Make a cross-shaped incision on the flat side of each chestnut, then boil in water for 15 - 20 minutes. Remove the skins whilst still hot.

This is an ideal festive dish for vegetarians – delicious with Casseroled Red Cabbage (see recipe p204) and Potato & Celeriac Dauphinoise (see recipe p192) or Stewed Leeks (see recipe p203).

Method

1. Preheat the oven to 200°C (gas mark 6). Line a large baking tray with baking parchment and set aside.

2. To make the filling, put the brazil nuts and chestnuts into the bowl of a food processor and, using the pulse button, process until they are roughly chopped. Remove and set aside in a large mixing bowl.

3. Melt the butter in a large, heavy-based saucepan over a moderate heat. Add the onion and cook until softened but not coloured. Next add the mushrooms, garlic and thyme and continue to cook until all the juice from the mushrooms has evaporated. Allow to cool a little, then transfer to the food processor. Again, using the pulse button, process carefully so that the mixture is roughly chopped but does not become sloppy. Add the mushroom mixture to the brazil nuts and chestnuts in the mixing bowl.

Ingredients

Serves 6 - 8

100g brazil nuts

200g cooked chestnuts

25g butter

1 small onion, finely chopped

300g button mushrooms, finely sliced

1 large garlic clove, crushed

1 teaspoon fresh thyme leaves

25g fresh breadcrumbs

25g poppy seeds

1 small egg, lightly beaten

salt & freshly ground black pepper

350g puff pastry (recipe p230)

For the decoration

1 small egg, beaten

poppy seeds

Chestnut & Mushroom Roulade

4. Next add the breadcrumbs, poppy seeds and lightly beaten egg and combine together thoroughly. Finally, season with salt and freshly ground black pepper.

5. Roll out the puff pastry into a rectangle, half a centimetre in thickness, approximately 30cm in length and 25cm in width. Place the filling lengthways down the centre leaving a gap of 3cm at each end. With a sharp knife, make 10 - 12 diagonal cuts down each side of the pastry, then brush with the beaten egg. Fold the top and bottom ends of the pastry over the filling, then starting at the top plait the cut strands of pastry over one another.

6. Transfer the roulade to the baking tray. Brush with the remaining beaten egg and sprinkle with poppy seeds. Place in the preheated oven for 20 minutes, then reduce the temperature to 175°C (gas mark 3½) and bake for approximately 10 - 15 more minutes until the pastry is cooked through and golden brown. Serve warm.

Ingredients

Serves approximately 6

1kg parsnips, peeled and cut into pieces lengthways

150g plain white flour

50g Parmesan cheese, freshly grated

salt & freshly ground black pepper

sunflower oil

PARSNIPS

Parsnips were highly prized in Roman times and continued to be the pre-eminent winter root vegetable in Europe until the introduction of the potato in the 18th century. Because of their high natural sugar content parsnips can be used in both sweet and savoury dishes. They are also a rich winter source of vitamin C, potassium and folacin.

Roasted Parsnips

The grated Parmesan cheese in this recipe gives the sweet flesh of the parsnips a crisp savoury coating. They can be prepared several hours in advance and finished in the oven as required.

Method

1. Preheat the oven to 200°C (gas mark 6). Mix the flour, Parmesan, salt and pepper together in a medium-sized bowl.

2. Put the parsnips into a large, heavy-based pan, cover with salted water, bring to the boil and cook for 3 - 4 minutes. Drain, and whilst still steaming, toss the hot parsnips in the flour and Parmesan mixture, several at a time, until they are well coated.

3. To finish the parsnips, cover the base of a large roasting tin with sunflower oil and preheat in the oven for a couple of minutes. Add the prepared parsnips, turning them so that they are all well basted with the hot oil. Roast in the oven for approximately 20 minutes, then turn them and roast for a further 20 minutes until they are crisp and browned.

Orange-glazed Carrots

Carrots cooked in this way are really tasty. The butter, brown sugar and orange juice combine together to form a beautiful shiny glaze.

Method

1. Cut the carrots into even-sized chunks, 3 - 4cm in length, then put them into a heavy-based saucepan, together with the butter, salt, brown sugar and orange juice. Now add sufficient water to come two-thirds of the way up the carrots.

2. Bring to the boil over a medium heat, and cook until the liquid has almost evaporated. Turn down the heat and continue to cook, stirring occasionally, until a glaze has formed on the carrots. Season with pepper and sprinkle with the parsley.

Stewed Leeks

Method

1. Remove the outer leaves, trim the top and bottom, and clean the leeks thoroughly, making sure all the soil which gets trapped between the leaves has been removed.

2. Slice lengthways, then chop into pieces roughly 1½cm wide. Put in a heavy-based saucepan with a large knob of butter and place over a low heat. Allow to stew in their own juice for 10 - 15 minutes, until soft but not coloured. If desired, finish with a spoonful of cream and freshly ground black pepper.

Ingredients

Serves approximately 6

1kg medium-sized carrots, peeled

100g butter

1 teaspoon salt

2 heaped teaspoons brown sugar

8 tablespoons fresh orange juice

freshly ground black pepper

fresh parsley, chopped

LEEKS

A member of the allium family, leeks are one of the most useful winter vegetables in the kitchen, flavouring soups, stews and casseroles. They also help lower cholesterol levels, protecting against high blood pressure.

Ingredients

Serves 10

100g butter

1 large onion, finely chopped

2 garlic cloves, crushed

1 medium-sized red cabbage, roughly 1kg, finely shredded

4 medium eating apples, peeled, cored and finely sliced

grated zest and juice of 2 oranges

1 teaspoon mixed spice

2 tablespoons brown sugar

300ml red wine

2 tablespoons red wine vinegar

salt & freshly ground black pepper

RED CABBAGE

During the winter months, cabbages provide us with a rich source of nutrients, including potassium, manganese, folate, iron and vitamins B6, K and C.

Casseroled Red Cabbage

This recipe is a delicious combination of savoury and sweet. Rich in flavour and colour, it is the perfect winter accompaniment for roast meat or sausages. This dish reheats well and keeps for several months in the freezer.

Method

1. Melt the butter in a large, heavy-based saucepan or casserole. Add the onion and garlic and soften for a few minutes over a low heat taking care that they do not colour.

2. Next add the cabbage, stirring well to coat it with the butter. Add the apples, orange juice and zest, mixed spice, brown sugar, red wine, wine vinegar, salt and pepper.

3. Combine well, cover with a lid and simmer over a low heat for approximately 30 minutes. The apples should now be cooked through and the cabbage nice and tender. Remove the lid, adjust the seasoning if necessary and simmer for a further 10 minutes.

Savoy Cabbage

This is the best of all winter cabbages, with its crinkly leaves and sweet mild flavour.

Method

1. Shred the cabbage finely, then toss in a heavy-based saucepan with a little butter, salt and freshly ground black pepper.
2. Stir constantly until it becomes slightly translucent but still retains some crunch. Serve immediately.

SAVOY CABBAGE

In addition to containing high levels of vitamin C, B₆ and K, savoy cabbage contains five times the quantity of beta-carotene than other cabbage varieties. In the Middle Ages, seafaring explorers discovered that eating cabbage whilst at sea would prevent them from getting scurvy.

Roasted Carrots & Beetroot

These two tasty, slightly sweet root vegetables are delicious roasted together. The colour from the beetroot tinges the carrots a delicate pink.

Method

1. Preheat the oven to 180°C (gas mark 4). Peel the carrots and beetroots and chop into chunks. Lay in a roasting tin, drizzle with extra virgin olive oil and sprinkle with salt and freshly ground black pepper.
2. Place in the oven for 30 - 35 minutes, until slightly browned and tender.

BEETROOT

This spherical, deeply pigmented root vegetable is believed to have ancient origins, growing wild over most of the northern hemisphere. Originally only the leaves were eaten but eventually, the sweet flavour of the root became appreciated in its own right.

Christmas Pudding

This is the recipe that my mother makes every year for our Christmas dinner, and I have yet to taste a better pudding. In our family, we keep the tradition of hiding silver charms inside – all of which have great significance for the approaching new year. Originally, these would have included silver threepenny pieces – if you were lucky enough to find one of those in your portion of pudding, without doubt you were about to make your fortune.

Christmas puddings are traditionally made on the 'Sunday before Advent' – that is five weeks before Christmas. The collect in the Book of Common Prayer for that day begins "Stir up, we beseech thee O Lord…"; therefore, it has become known as 'stir up Sunday'. All the members of the family would take it in turn to stir the pudding mixture, making a silent wish for the new year.

Although, traditionally, beef suet would have been used, the recipe works equally well with vegetable suet. If you like a spicy pudding, add ¼ teaspoon of cinnamon and nutmeg to the mixture. If adding charms, wrap them well in greaseproof paper before putting them in the mixture.

Method

1. Brush the inside of the pudding basin liberally with the softened butter.

2. Place all the dry ingredients together in a large mixing bowl. In another bowl combine the lightly beaten eggs with the ale and brandy or rum. Pour the egg and ale mixture into the dry mix then stir well until thoroughly combined.

3. Spoon into the prepared pudding basin and cover the surface of the mixture with a circle of greaseproof paper. Take a piece of tin foil larger than the top of the pudding basin, lay it over the top, shiny side down, and smooth the edges down the sides of the bowl to seal it.

Ingredients

For a 17cm diameter,
1 litre pudding basin
Serves approximately 10

soft butter for greasing the pudding basin

350g seedless raisins

125g currants

125g mixed peel (orange, lemon and citron), chopped

125g naturally coloured glacé cherries

50g blanched almonds, chopped

160g fine breadcrumbs

160g chopped suet (beef or vegetable)

4 large eggs, lightly beaten

100ml brown ale or stout

3 tablespoons brandy or rum

Christmas Pudding

DRIED VINE FRUITS

Currants, raisins and sultanas are grapes which have been preserved by drying. In some countries the fruit is laid between the rows of vines for approximately three weeks to dry in the sun, in others the process is carried out mechanically. The dried fruit contains concentrated natural sugars and will keep well for many months.

Ingredients

Makes approximately 1.2 litres

110g butter

50g plain white flour

1 litre milk

75g demerara sugar

110ml rum

125ml whipping cream

4. Take a saucepan large enough to hold the pudding basin easily. Next, take a large piece of tin foil – approximately 60cm in length. Fold it lengthways several times so that it is roughly 10cm in width. Fashion it into a sling around the base of the pudding so that you can lower the basin into the pan holding the two ends, leaving it in place while the pudding steams. Add enough water to come halfway up the sides of the pudding basin. Cover with a lid and simmer over a moderate heat. Steam for approximately 7 hours, remembering to top up the water if necessary.

5. Remove from the heat and leave to cool down for a few minutes. Using the tin foil sling, lift the pudding out of the pan and set aside to cool completely. Keep covered and store in a cool place until required.

6. To serve, place the pudding (complete with tin foil sling) back in the saucepan and steam for a further 2 hours. Turn out onto a large plate, pour a little brandy or rum over the top and ignite. Serve immediately. Delicious with Rum Sauce (see recipe below).

Rum Sauce

Method

1. Melt the butter slowly in a heavy-based saucepan. Add the flour and stir. Place over a low heat for a minute until pale and bubbling.

2. Bit by bit add the milk, stirring continuously until thickened. Add the sugar and continue to stir whilst cooking over a low heat for a further 5 minutes.

3. Remove from the stove and stir in the rum and whipping cream.

Syllabub Trifle

This is the most extravagant of desserts, perfect for a celebration. It is also a lovely alternative to Christmas Pudding.

Start the trifle 2 – 3 days before you wish to serve it. There are four stages to the recipe – each requiring cooling and refrigeration.

The bottom layer is made from moist, chewy almond macaroons soaked in a mixture of brandy and wine. Italian amaretti biscuits can be used as an alternative, but because of their dry texture the quantity of wine will need to be increased accordingly.

The final layer of the trifle is a generously alcoholic syllabub which can be made as a dessert in its own right, served in individual glasses.

Method

1. Press the macaroons into the base of a deep glass bowl so that they form a solid layer. Pour the dessert wine and brandy over the top and leave in a cool place for several hours to allow the liquid to be absorbed. Next, spread a thick layer of raspberry jam over the surface of the macaroons and place in the fridge to cool for several hours.

2. Next make the custard. Put the eggs, egg yolks and cornflour in a bowl and beat them together with a hand whisk until smooth. Bring the single cream to the boil in a medium-sized, heavy-based saucepan, stirring well to avoid it catching on the bottom. Pour it over the egg mixture whilst continuing to whisk. Return the mixture to the pan and place over a low heat, stirring with the hand whisk constantly until it is thick enough to coat the back of a wooden spoon. Take great care at this stage – if the custard cooks too quickly it will coagulate and resemble scrambled eggs. If this should happen, pass it through a fine sieve or beat it very vigorously with the hand whisk.

Ingredients

Serves 10 – 12

- 10 large almond macaroons
- 140ml white dessert wine
- 50ml brandy
- approximately 4 - 5 tablespoons best-quality raspberry jam

For the custard

- 2 large eggs
- 2 large egg yolks
- 1 heaped tablespoon cornflour
- 570ml single cream
- caster sugar to taste

For the syllabub

- 140ml sherry
- 30ml brandy
- juice of 1 lemon
- 50g caster sugar
- 290ml double cream
- a scraping of freshly grated nutmeg

For the decoration

- small ratafia biscuits
- flaked or strip almonds, toasted
- whole candied lemon peel, cut into small slivers
- crystallised angelica, cut into small strips

Syllabub Trifle

3. Add caster sugar to taste – bearing in mind the sweetness of the macaroons. Leave to cool a little, then spoon the thickened custard carefully over the jam. Allow to cool completely then return to the fridge and leave overnight to set.

4. Next, make the syllabub. Put the sherry, brandy and lemon juice in a large mixing bowl, then add the sugar and stir until it has completely dissolved. Whilst still stirring add the double cream and nutmeg. Then beat the mixture with a hand whisk until it just holds its shape – if overbeaten the cream will curdle and separate. Pour the syllabub over the set custard and spread evenly. Return to the fridge and leave overnight.

5. Decorate the trifle delicately with the miniature ratafia biscuits, toasted flaked almonds, slivers of candied peel and strips of angelica.

ANGELICA

Although well known for its medicinal properties, particularly in the treatment of digestive disorders and blood circulation, these days angelica is more frequently used as a culinary plant. The stalks are harvested, crystallised in sugar and used as decorations for cakes and puddings. This statuesque plant grows in our kitchen garden – it is also possible to find angelica growing wild in moist, shady places throughout Britain.

Mincemeat

Mincemeat, as the name suggests, originally contained minced meat. In ancient times when meat was preserved by many different means, one of the tastier methods was to mix it with fruit, spices and alcohol. It is said that King Henry V was so keen on mincemeat that he was served a mince pie at his coronation in 1413. This rather special recipe, which contains several unusual and interesting ingredients, was given to me by my mother. It is easy to make, and so superior to anything that can be bought in a shop.

Method

1. Sterilise your jars and lids by preheating the oven to 180°C (gas mark 4). Wash the jars and lids in hot soapy water and then rinse – do not dry with a tea towel. Place them on a baking sheet and leave in the oven for at least 10 minutes. Remove and allow to cool completely before filling.

2. Place all the dry ingredients together in a large mixing bowl and combine well. Mix the lemon and orange juice together in a jug, add the rum or brandy and pour into the dry ingredients. Stir well, then pack into the prepared jars and store in a cool place. Mincemeat should keep for at least 6 months.

Ingredients

Makes approximately 3 medium-sized jars

55g blanched almonds, chopped

110g whole candied peel (orange, lemon and citron), finely chopped

1 medium 'Bramley' apple, peeled and finely chopped

200g shredded suet (beef or vegetable)

55g naturally coloured glacé cherries, chopped

25g crystallised ginger, chopped

25g glacé pineapple, chopped

225g seedless raisins

225g currants

225g sultanas

175g soft light-brown sugar

¼ teaspoon salt

¼ teaspoon freshly grated nutmeg

¼ teaspoon ground mixed spice

grated zest and juice of ½ lemon

grated zest and juice of ½ orange

150ml rum or brandy

Ingredients

Makes 12 – 15, depending on size and shape, or one large 28cm tart

500g sweet pastry (recipe p232)

1 – 2 jars home-made Mincemeat (recipe p213)

icing sugar

Mince Pies

A mince pie can be a tiny tasty mouthful or a large family-sized tart, decorated simply with a pastry star or covered with a crunchy layer of streusel crumble (see recipe p39). A topping of rich almond frangipane (see recipe p169) transforms it into a sophisticated festive dessert, especially if served warm with home-made Brandy Butter (see recipe opposite). If making a large tart, it is advisable to blind bake the pastry case before filling, as in the Walnut Tart recipe (see p167).

Method

1. First make the sweet pastry as described on p232. Remove from the fridge and allow to almost reach room temperature. Lightly dust the work surface and rolling pin with flour, then roll the pastry out, lightly but firmly, until it is approximately 3mm thick. Line the mince pie tins, then cut out circles or stars from the remaining pastry to cover the tops of the pies. Place in the fridge to rest for at least 20 minutes. Preheat the oven to 180°C (gas mark 4).

2. Remove from the fridge and spoon the mincemeat into the pastry cases, cover with the prepared tops and place in the preheated oven. Baking time will vary depending on the size of the pies – small ones will take approximately 15 – 20 minutes, a large tart covered with frangipane will need 45 – 50 minutes. Once removed from the oven, leave to cool slightly. Before serving, dust with icing sugar.

Mulled Wine

A deliciously warming festive drink. Serve with Mince Pies (see recipe opposite), Christmas Cake (see recipe p219), or enjoy it just on its own on a very cold day.

Method

1. Place all the ingredients in a large, heavy-based saucepan. Heat slowly to simmering point, then reduce to a low heat for 20 minutes – do not allow to come to the boil or the alcohol will evaporate.

2. Strain and serve immediately, or allow to cool naturally and store in the refrigerator until required.

Brandy Butter

This will keep for several weeks in the fridge.

Method

1. Place the butter in a mixing bowl and beat with a spoon until white and creamy.

2. Beat the icing sugar gradually into the butter, sifting it through a sieve to remove any lumps. Next add the brandy and lemon juice, a little at a time until completely incorporated.

3. Transfer to a butter dish and place in the fridge to set for at least 2 hours before serving.

Ingredients

Serves approximately 10

1½ litres red wine

8 fresh orange slices

6 fresh lemon slices

2 cinnamon sticks

8 cloves

165g caster sugar

Ingredients

Makes approximately 500g

250g butter, at room temperature

250g icing sugar

50ml brandy

1 teaspoon freshly squeezed lemon juice

Lebkuchen Tree Hangings

These continental tree hangings are both pretty and tasty. There are never any left on our Christmas tree by the end of the Christmas festivities.

Method

1. Preheat the oven to 180°C (gas mark 4). Line a large baking tray with baking parchment. Place the golden syrup, treacle, brown sugar, spices and water in a large, heavy-based pan. Stir well over a low heat, then gradually bring to the boil. Remove and allow to cool slightly.

2. Sprinkle the baking powder and bicarbonate of soda into the mixture and stir until dissolved. Add the butter and whisk until it has completely melted.

3. Place the flour in a large mixing bowl and add the syrup mixture. Combine together until a smooth, soft paste has formed. Don't overwork, and don't worry if it is a little sloppy at this stage – it will become firm as it cools.

4. When completely cold, dust the work surface with a little flour and roll out the paste until it is approximately 5mm thick. Cut out the shapes of your choice, remembering to make a hole at the top of each one for the ribbon (a drinking straw is a good tool for this job).

5. Lay on the prepared baking tray and bake for approximately 20 minutes, until firm and a little browned. Leave to cool on a cooling rack.

6. Make the water icing by mixing the water and icing sugar together. Brush the cold biscuits with the icing, then, when almost dry, dust with icing sugar. Thread a ribbon through the hole in each – they are now ready to hang on the Christmas tree.

Ingredients

Makes 10 - 12

70g golden syrup

1 dessertspoon black treacle

70g soft light-brown sugar

a pinch each of ground cinnamon, mixed spice, ground ginger and freshly grated nutmeg

1 tablespoon water

a pinch each of baking powder and bicarbonate of soda

100g butter, cut into small pieces

225g plain white flour, sieved

For the water icing

140g icing sugar

4 dessertspoons water

Christmas Cake

This recipe has been handed down to me by my mother. It makes a beautifully moist and colourful cake which I like to decorate with glacé fruits.

Method

1. Line the bottom and sides of a 20cm diameter cake tin with baking parchment. Preheat the oven to 140°C (gas mark 1).

2. Place the butter and sugar together in a large mixing bowl. Beat until pale and creamy.

3. Add the eggs, one by one, mixing in well.

4. Combine the flour, almonds and salt together and add to the mixture gradually.

5. Next, add the sultanas, pineapple, ginger, peel, angelica, walnuts, sherry and lemon juice and zest. Mix well, then gently stir in the cherries so that they remain whole.

6. Transfer the cake mixture to the cake tin, flattening the surface with a spatula. Bake in the preheated oven for approximately 3 hours. The cake will be ready when it is golden brown on top and firm to the touch, but don't be afraid to give it a little longer if it doesn't appear to be ready. To check, pierce the centre with a thin skewer – it should come out clean.

7. When cool enough to handle, remove from the cake tin and leave on a cooling rack until completely cold. To store, wrap in tin foil and place in an airtight container in a cool place.

8. To decorate, place the apricot jam and water in a small pan over a low heat. Stir well until you have a thick glaze. Brush the top of the cake with a generous quantity of the apricot mixture, then lay the glacé fruits on top in a design of your choice. Allow to cool, then brush the top of the fruits with a little more apricot glaze.

Ingredients

Makes a 20cm diameter cake

- 250g butter, at room temperature
- 250g caster sugar
- 4 large eggs
- 250g plain white flour
- 75g ground almonds
- pinch of salt
- 250g golden sultanas
- 125g glacé pineapple, finely chopped
- 75g crystallised ginger, finely chopped
- 185g whole mixed peel (lemon, orange and citron), finely chopped
- 50g angelica, finely chopped
- 125g chopped walnuts
- 50ml sherry
- grated zest and juice of 1 lemon
- 250g naturally coloured glacé cherries

For the decoration

- 3 - 4 tablespoons apricot jam
- 3 - 4 tablespoons water
- glacé fruits (orange and lemon slices, pineapple, apricots, figs, cherries, angelica)

Chestnut & Hazelnut Cake

The recipe for this beautifully moist cake comes from Switzerland where sweet chestnut trees grow in profusion, particularly in the south of the country around the lakes of Maggiore and Lugano. Because it is so rich, I prefer not to decorate it with icing – a light dusting of cocoa powder just finishes it off.

The texture of the cake improves if it is kept for a day or two to mature before being eaten – it also keeps well in the freezer for several weeks. For a gluten free version, substitute the flour with the equivalent weight of extra ground almonds.

Method

1. Preheat the oven to 175°C (gas mark 3½). Line the base and sides of a 20cm diameter cake tin (preferably springform or loose-bottomed) with baking parchment, using a little melted butter to keep it in place.

2. Separate the eggs, putting the whites to one side. Put the yolks and one half of the caster sugar in a large mixing bowl. Whisk together until pale and creamy and doubled in volume. Mix in the chestnut purée, then fold in the flour, sifting it through a sieve. Finally, gently stir in the ground and chopped hazelnuts followed by the ground almonds.

3. Place the egg whites in a clean bowl and whisk thoroughly until they form soft peaks. Add the remaining sugar and continue to beat until thick and glossy. With a large metal spoon, stir a little of the egg-white mixture into the nut mixture to slacken it, then gently fold in the remainder of the egg-white mixture.

4. Spoon into the prepared cake tin and place in the preheated oven for approximately 50 - 55 minutes until firm to the touch and golden brown. To test, pierce with a clean skewer – if it comes out clean, the cake is ready. Allow to cool completely before sprinkling with cocoa powder. Delicious with a dollop of whipped cream or crème fraîche.

Ingredients

Makes a 20cm diameter cake

4 large eggs

280g caster sugar, divided into 2 halves

200g chestnut purée

100g plain white flour

100g ground hazelnuts

50g chopped hazelnuts

50g ground almonds

cocoa powder for dusting

CHESTNUTS

In many of the areas in Switzerland and Italy that are covered with sweet chestnut forests, the nuts are dried and ground into flour which is used in baking through the winter months. Chestnuts are low in both fat and calories, high in vitamin C and potassium, and also contain significant amounts of vitamin B.

Chocolate Panettone Pudding

This recipe, which can be prepared 24 hours in advance, will work perfectly well with brioche or a humble loaf of white bread, but panettone makes it really special. Use chocolate with a high cocoa-solid content, preferably over 60%, otherwise the pudding will be very sweet.

Method

1. Cut the panettone into slices roughly 1cm thick, then cut each slice into rectangles approximately 9cm by 5cm. Stand the prepared slices on their longest side in a large ovenproof serving dish, leaning them against each other until the whole dish is full.

2. Find a large heatproof bowl which will fit comfortably over the top of a saucepan. If the bowl is too large for the pan, it will move about too much – if it is too small it will hang too low in the pan. Cover the bottom of the pan with water, making sure it does not touch the underside of the bowl. Bring to the boil and simmer gently.

3. Put the chocolate, cream, sugar, butter, cinnamon and rum together in the bowl and place over the top of the simmering pan. Stir occasionally, until the chocolate and butter have melted completely. Carefully lift the bowl and contents off the top of the pan, then whisk the beaten eggs into the chocolate mixture. Pour the chocolate mixture evenly over the top of the panettone slices and leave to stand for several hours in a cool place.

4. Preheat the oven to 170°C (gas mark 3). Slide the ovenproof dish onto a baking tray and place in the preheated oven for approximately 30 - 35 minutes. It will have risen and be slightly crispy on the top when it is ready. After removing from the oven, allow to stand for several minutes before serving. Decorate the top with icing sugar sprinkled through a small strainer. Serve with fresh cream or crème fraîche.

Ingredients

Serves 8

approximately 600g panettone (roughly one large one)

275g best-quality plain dark chocolate, broken into small pieces

725ml whipping cream

165g caster sugar

125g unsalted butter

large pinch of ground cinnamon

6 tablespoons rum

6 eggs, beaten

icing sugar for decoration

Pears Poached in Red Wine

For this recipe, you will need a good firm variety of pear, such as 'Conference', and decent quality red wine.

During the poaching, the pears absorb the wine and take on a jewel-like colour. Serve them in their own spicy red wine syrup with a dollop of lightly whipped cream. They can be prepared in advance and kept in the fridge for up to 24 hours.

Method

1. Find a heavy-based saucepan just large enough to take all the pears, standing up side by side. Pour the red wine into the empty pan, then add the sugar, lemon peel, cinnamon and peppercorns. Place over a moderate heat, stirring well until the sugar has completely dissolved. Allow to boil for 5 minutes then remove from the heat.

2. Peel the pears neatly from the base upwards towards the stalk, then rub with the cut side of the lemon to prevent discolouration. Insert a small sharp knife in the base of each pear to remove the core, taking care not to pierce the top of the fruit, leaving the stalk in place. Flatten off the base of each pear by removing a thin slice, then fit them snugly into the pan, immersing them in the syrup – add a little more wine if necessary.

3. Cover the pan with a lid and return to the heat. Gradually bring to the boil, then simmer gently for 20 - 40 minutes until tender. The cooking time will depend on the variety, size and ripeness of the fruit. Remove from the heat and leave to cool for a few minutes.

4. Remove the pears from the pan with a slotted spoon and arrange in a serving dish. Pass the liquid through a strainer to remove the peppercorns and lemon peel and return to the pan. Place over the heat and boil rapidly until reduced by half and thickened to a syrup. Allow to cool slightly, then spoon over the pears. Chill thoroughly before serving.

Ingredients

Serves 8

8 firm-fleshed pears

approximately 1 litre red wine

100g caster sugar

2 strips of lemon peel

1 stick of cinnamon, approximately 5cm in length

1 teaspoon black peppercorns, tied in a piece of muslin

½ a lemon

PEARS

Pears are close relatives of both apples and quinces. They are sweet and delicate in flavour with a slightly gritty texture. We grow 'Conference' pears in our garden, which have a good, firm consistency and are sweet and juicy when ripe.

Chocolate Truffles

Home-made truffles are not only a luxurious indulgence at the end of a special meal – they also make a delicious gift.

This recipe uses dark chocolate, preferably over 60% cocoa solids, which is then combined with scalded cream to create a 'ganache' – a term that has French origins, literally meaning 'cushion'. Ganache is believed to have been invented in Switzerland in the middle of the 19th century, and to have acquired its name because of its resemblance to a soft, plush cushion, melting in the mouth.

Start this recipe the day before the truffles are required. They will keep in the fridge for several days.

Method

1. Chop the chocolate into tiny pieces and put into a bowl.

2. In a heavy-based saucepan, bring the double cream to boiling point and pour over the chocolate, stirring well until the chocolate has completely melted. Add any flavourings and combine well. Leave to cool naturally at room temperature.

3. When completely cold, beat with an electric hand mixer until it has the texture of stiffly whipped cream. Leave to stand in a cool place overnight – this allows the cocoa butter in the chocolate to crystallise, so that when the ganache is shaped or eaten it melts more slowly.

4. To shape the truffles, using a small teaspoon, divide the mixture into rough balls of the desired size, leave them to set in the fridge for 20 minutes.

5. With the minimum of handling, form the cooled balls into spheres and roll in the covering of your choice.

Ingredients

Makes roughly 3 dozen truffles, depending on size

- 250g best-quality plain dark chocolate

- 125ml double cream

- flavourings: 1 teaspoon of either vanilla extract, Cointreau, Kirsch, cognac, finely chopped almonds or hazelnuts

- coverings: icing sugar, cocoa powder, grated chocolate, ground almonds or hazelnuts

The Pantry

Recipes

Ingredients

Makes approximately 550g

225g plain white flour

**3 pinches of salt
(or 1 if using salted butter)**

15g chilled butter, diced

90 - 140ml ice-cold water

**225g butter, at room
temperature, but not too
soft**

Puff Pastry

Puff pastry is both time-consuming and tricky to make. Prepare it the day before you need it, allowing plenty of time for resting between each stage.

Use the best-quality butter available, either salted or unsalted – freshness and flavour are of the most importance. If using salted butter, reduce the quantity of salt added to the flour at the beginning of the recipe. Equal weights of butter and flour are needed – make sure that the butter is firm but not too solid or it will be difficult to roll.

The water should be as cold as possible – preferably icy. If at any stage the pastry becomes elastic or butter starts to come through the surface, wrap it in cling film and leave it to rest in the fridge for 10 minutes.

It is important to keep the sides of the pastry straight and at right angles to one another, otherwise it will not retain its rectangular shape and will be difficult to fold. When rolling, try to avoid pushing movements with the rolling pin as this will move the butter out of place. Instead, bring the rolling pin down firmly onto the pastry and give a quick short roll, lightly but firmly back and forth. Repeat down the length of the pastry, creating a series of ridges. Follow this with a light roll away from you, never from side to side.

Puff pastry will keep for 2 - 3 days in the fridge or 2 months in the freezer.

Method

1. Sieve the flour into a large mixing bowl. Add the salt, then rub in the diced cold butter. Next add the cold water, a little at a time whilst stirring with the blade of a knife until clumps of dough have formed. Using your hands, pull the clumps together and fold over 4 or 5 times to make a firm but pliable dough. This is known as the détrempe.

   Remove from the bowl and place on a lightly floured surface. Shape into a rectangle approximately 10cm by 15cm, then wrap in cling film and leave to rest in a cool place for 30 minutes.

2. The remaining butter needs to be the same consistency as the détrempe. If it is too firm, place between two pieces of greaseproof paper and beat with the rolling pin several times to make it more pliable. Roll the détrempe into a rectangle approximately 15cm by 30cm. The slab of butter should be slightly less than half the size of the détrempe. Place the butter in the centre of one half of the dough. Fold the other half over and press the edges tightly together. Allow to rest for 15 minutes.

3. With the sealed ends towards you, begin to ridge, then roll the pastry away from you. When it measures roughly 12cm by 35cm, fold the bottom third of the pastry up and the top third down to give three layers. Press the edges gently with the rolling pin to seal them together. Turn the pastry round through 90° so that the open edge faces you, then roll and fold again. Cover and leave to rest in a cool place for 15 minutes. Repeat this whole process twice more, chilling in the fridge in between each of the two rolls and folds. Wrap tightly and place in the fridge for a minimum of 2 – 3 hours (preferably overnight), before using.

Ingredients

Makes approximately 500g

250g plain white flour

60g caster sugar

125g chilled butter, cut into small pieces

1 large egg, lightly beaten

Sweet Pastry

This rich pastry is perfect for lining flan dishes or tart cases.

Method

1. Keeping everything as cool as possible, place the flour, sugar and pieces of butter in a large mixing bowl and stir gently to coat the butter with the flour. Using your hands, begin to rub the butter gently into the flour and sugar, allowing it to fall between your fingers from a short height above the bowl – this will incorporate air into your pastry, making it light and crisp. As you work, the mixture should begin to resemble fine breadcrumbs.

2. When all of the butter has been worked into the flour and sugar, make a well in the centre and gradually add the beaten egg. Draw the mixture together until it has formed a dough. Take care not to overwork it – this will develop the gluten in the flour and the pastry will shrink back when baked.

3. Turn the pastry out onto a floured work surface, shape into a ball, wrap in cling film and leave to rest in the fridge for at least 30 minutes before using. Alternatively, store in a freezer for up to 2 months.

Simple Shortcrust Pastry

Simple shortcrust pastry is ideal for savoury flans and quiches.

Method

1. Keeping everything as cool as possible, place the flour, salt and pieces of butter in a large mixing bowl and stir gently to coat the butter with the flour. Rub the butter into the flour between your thumb and fingertips, allowing it to fall between your fingers from a short height above the bowl – this will incorporate air into your pastry, making it light and crisp.

2. When the mixture resembles fine breadcrumbs, sprinkle two tablespoons of cold water over the surface, then stir with the blade of a knife – the pastry will begin to form into lumps. Very gradually add more water, bringing the pastry together with your hands to form a dough. Take care not to overwork it – this will develop the gluten in the flour and the pastry will shrink back when baked.

3. Turn the pastry out onto a floured work surface, shape into a ball, wrap in cling film and chill in the fridge for at least 30 minutes before using.
   Alternatively, store in a freezer for up to 2 months.

Ingredients

Makes approximately 425g

250g plain white flour

pinch of salt

125g chilled butter, cut into small pieces

approximately 3 - 4 tablespoons ice-cold water

Ingredients

Makes approximately 450g

225g wholemeal flour

2 teaspoons baking powder

large pinch of salt

100g chilled butter, cut into small pieces

2 teaspoons soft light-brown sugar

3 - 4 tablespoons ice-cold water

2 tablespoons sunflower oil

Wholewheat Pastry

Wholewheat pastry can be hard and uninteresting – the baking powder and brown sugar give this version a light texture and nutty flavour.

Method

1. Keeping everything as cool as possible, mix the flour, baking powder and salt together in a large bowl. Add the butter, stirring gently to coat it with the flour. Begin to incorporate the pieces of butter into the flour mixture by lifting it above the bowl and rubbing it between your thumbs and fingertips as gently as possible, allowing it to fall through your hands. This will incorporate air into the pastry, making it light and 'short'. Continue until the mixture resembles fine breadcrumbs and all the lumps of butter have disappeared.

2. In a small jug, dissolve the sugar in the cold water and add the oil, stirring well. Add gradually to the flour mixture, stirring with a spoon until a dough is formed – you may not need to add all the liquid.

3. Turn the pastry out onto a floured work surface and shape into a ball. Take care not to overwork it – this will develop the gluten in the flour and the pastry will shrink back when baked. Wrap in cling film and place in the fridge to rest for at least 30 minutes before using.
Alternatively, store in a freezer for up to 2 months.

Marzipan

Although marzipan is readily available in the shops, it really is worth making your own. Shop-bought tends to be dry, flavourless and artificially coloured – home-made is rich, moist and incredibly delicious. It is also extremely easy to make.

Method

1. Mix all the dry ingredients together in a large mixing bowl. Add the sherry or rum, orange flower water, lemon juice and vanilla extract.

2. Gradually add the beaten eggs whilst working the ingredients together to form a stiff paste – you may find you do not need to add all of the egg.

3. Lightly dust the work surface with icing sugar, and knead the marzipan until smooth.

4. If not being used immediately, wrap in tin foil and store in the fridge for up to 2 weeks.

Ingredients

Makes approximately 1kg

250g icing sugar

250g caster sugar

500g ground almonds

2 dessertspoons sherry or rum

2 teaspoons orange flower water

2 dessertspoons freshly squeezed lemon juice

a few drops of vanilla extract

2 medium eggs, lightly beaten

ORANGE FLOWER WATER

This rather old fashioned ingredient is a natural extract, made directly from the distillation of orange blossoms. It is highly perfumed and can be used in desserts and puddings. Several drops in gin and vermouth makes a perfect Victorian martini.

Ingredients

Makes approximately 1 litre

roughly 1kg of bones

2 litres cold water

2 onions, diced

1 carrot, peeled and chopped

2 sticks of celery, sliced

1 leek, chopped

55g mushrooms

2 - 3 stalks of fresh parsley

1 bay leaf

1 sprig of fresh thyme

½ teaspoon black peppercorns

THYME

Thyme is native to North Africa and the Mediterranean, where it grows wild in great profusion. It has a fresh, slightly peppery flavour which adds subtle character to soups, stews and casseroles. This variegated variety, 'Silver Queen', which grows in our garden is also highly decorative.

Meat Stock

Meat stock can be made from the bones of chicken, veal, beef or lamb.

Method

1. Place the bones in a deep, heavy-based pan. Cover with the water and bring to a simmer. Skim off any fat or scum that rises to the surface with a metal spoon.

2. When the water begins to boil properly, remove the pan from the heat and add a further cupful of cold water – this will solidify the fat and make it easy to remove. The remaining liquid should now be clear.

3. Add the rest of the ingredients and return the pan to the heat. Simmer gently for 3 - 4 hours, adding more water if necessary to keep all the ingredients covered. Skim the surface occasionally, if required.

4. Once the stock is cooked, strain it carefully through a fine sieve and store in the fridge as soon as it is sufficiently cool. Stock will keep for 3 days in the fridge, or for 6 months in the freezer.

Vegetable Stock

Method

1. Place all the ingredients in a large, heavy-based saucepan and simmer gently for 30 minutes. Remove any scum that rises to the surface with a metal spoon.

2. Strain through a fine sieve and allow to cool completely before storing in the fridge for up to 3 days. Alternatively, store in the freezer for up to 6 months.

Ingredients

Makes approximately 1 litre

2 onions, diced

2 carrots, peeled and chopped

1 leek, chopped

2 sticks of celery, sliced

2 - 3 dried mushrooms or several fresh ones

2 garlic cloves, roughly chopped

2 litres cold water

3 - 4 stalks of fresh parsley

2 sprigs of fresh thyme

1 sprig of fresh rosemary

2 bay leaves

½ teaspoon black peppercorns

salt

GARLIC

Garlic is extremely pungent if used raw but the longer it is cooked, the milder the flavour will be.

Ingredients

Makes approximately 250ml

- 2 tablespoons freshly squeezed lemon juice
- 1 tablespoon white wine vinegar
- 175g butter
- 3 egg yolks
- 1 teaspoon caster sugar
- pinch of salt

Ingredients

Makes approximately 250ml

- 1 quantity of hollandaise sauce (recipe above)
- 3 - 4 tablespoons fresh tarragon, chopped

Hollandaise Sauce

Using a hand blender may not be the orthodox way of making hollandaise, but it is quick, easy and gives reliable results.

Method

1. Place the lemon juice and wine vinegar in one small saucepan and the butter in another. Put the egg yolks, caster sugar and salt in a jug or the hand blender goblet.

2. Heat the lemon juice and vinegar until it is just bubbling and the butter until it is completely melted and almost boiling. Using the hand blender, whizz the eggs, sugar and salt together for a few seconds then, whilst still whizzing, gradually add the bubbling lemon juice and vinegar followed by the foaming butter – a beautiful, rich smooth hollandaise should result. Covered, it will keep in the fridge for 4 - 5 days. Serve with artichokes (see p89), asparagus (see p29) or hot Salmon en Papillote (see recipe p86).

Béarnaise Sauce

Delicious with chicken, beef and other roasted meats.

Method

1. Follow the instructions above, for hollandaise sauce.
2. When blended, stir in the fresh tarragon.

Mayonnaise

Mayonnaise is an emulsion of lemon juice, oil and raw egg yolk. It is believed to have been invented in Mahón, the capital of Menorca, one of the Balearic islands – hence the name. To make aïoli, the Provençal version of mayonnaise, add a couple of cloves of crushed fresh garlic to the egg yolks at the start of the process.

The ingredients need to be at room temperature – if they are cold, warm the bowl a little. If the mayonnaise separates, beat it gradually, teaspoon by teaspoon into another egg yolk. An electric hand whisk is a great help.

Method

1. Place the egg yolks, mustard powder, sugar, salt and ½ a tablespoon of the lemon juice in a bowl and whisk together vigorously for at least one minute.

2. Continuing to whisk, dribble the oil into the mixture very gradually – it should begin to emulsify and thicken. Continue until roughly a third of the oil has been incorporated.

3. Now add the remaining lemon juice gradually, whisking continuously, followed by the remaining oil – you should now have a thick glossy mayonnaise. Perfect with vegetable sticks, salads or Salmon en Papillote (see recipe p86). Store in the fridge, covered, for up to 1 week.

Ingredients

Makes approximately 500ml

2 egg yolks

½ teaspoon dry English mustard powder

½ teaspoon caster sugar

½ teaspoon salt

3½ tablespoons freshly squeezed lemon juice

350ml mild flavoured olive oil

Ingredients

Makes approximately 450ml

100ml white wine vinegar

3 level teaspoons Dijon
mustard

2 garlic cloves, crushed

salt & freshly ground
black pepper

300ml extra virgin olive oil

Ingredients

Makes approximately 450ml

150ml extra virgin olive oil

150ml grape seed oil

100ml white wine vinegar

1 teaspoon smooth mustard

1 teaspoon caster sugar

2 tablespoons whipping
cream

salt & freshly ground
black pepper

Ingredients

Makes 400ml

300ml extra virgin olive oil

100ml aged balsamic
vinegar

freshly ground black pepper

French Dressing

Method

1. Whisk the vinegar and mustard together with the garlic, salt and freshly ground black pepper.

2. Whilst still whisking, gradually add the oil – the mixture should emulsify. Store in the fridge for up to 2 weeks.

Swiss Dressing

Method

1. Place all the ingredients together in a jug or small bowl. Blend together with a small whisk until creamy and emulsified. The dressing should not be too thick – if necessary, a little water can be added to give a light coating consistency. Store in the fridge for 2 – 3 days.

Balsamic Dressing

Method

1. Mix together the olive oil, balsamic vinegar and pepper, stirring well to amalgamate. Store in the fridge for 2 – 3 weeks.

Caramelised Red Onion Marmalade

Perfect with roasted meats, cheese and many other savoury dishes.

Method

1. Place the onions in a bowl with the salt and leave for at least 1 hour in the fridge. Rinse thoroughly and drain well.

2. Simmer the sugar and vinegar together in a large, heavy-based saucepan for 5 minutes, then add the onions and continue to simmer for 2 - 2½ hours, uncovered, until the mixture is thick and has the texture of marmalade. Transfer to a container and store in the fridge for up to 1 month.

Ingredients

Makes 2 small to medium jars

500g red onions, finely sliced

2 teaspoons salt

400g sugar

200ml red wine vinegar

RED ONIONS

Onions are the most useful vegetable in the kitchen. Originally cultivated over 5000 years ago, they have long been valued for their medicinal qualities and potent flavour. In addition to vitamins C and B6, they contain over 150 phytochemicals as well as quercetin – a substance which is known to block the formation of cancer cells. Research has also shown that compounds found in onions can kill infectious bacteria and help dissolve blood clots. This variety, grown in our garden, is 'Red Baron', which is mild and sweet – the perfect ingredient for Caramelised Red Onion Marmalade.

Ingredients

Makes 2 - 3 small jars

100g butter

300g light brown sugar

50g golden syrup

a few drops of vanilla extract

150ml milk

150ml single cream

Ingredients

Makes approximately 1 medium-sized jar

225g raspberries

juice of ½ lemon

icing sugar to taste

Toffee Sauce

This smooth buttery sauce is delicious with Vanilla Ice Cream (see recipe p105) or Pancakes (see recipe p43).

Method

1. Place the butter, sugar, golden syrup, vanilla extract and milk together in a small, heavy-based pan. Place over a moderate heat and bring to the boil. Continue to boil until the sauce thickens – about 5 minutes.

2. Remove from the heat and allow to cool slightly, then whilst still warm stir in the cream. When completely cool store in the fridge for up to 2 - 3 weeks.

Raspberry Sauce

Delicious with ice cream or as an accompaniment for Pavlova (see recipe p101), Caramelised Lemon Tart (see recipe p47), and many other puddings and desserts. Use fresh fruit for the best results, although frozen raspberries also work well.

Method

1. Liquidise the raspberries and lemon juice with a hand blender. Add several teaspoons of icing sugar to taste, then check for sweetness – the quantity required will depend on the tartness of the fruit.

2. Pass through a sieve to remove the pips. Pour into a jug if using immediately, or store in the fridge for up to 5 days.

Chocolate Sauce

This rich, velvety sauce can be warmed and poured over Vanilla Ice Cream (see recipe p105), profiteroles (see p72), or stirred into hot milk to create the perfect hot chocolate. Use plain dark chocolate with a high cocoa percentage – 60% or above if possible.

Method

1. Find a large heatproof bowl which will fit comfortably over the top of a saucepan. If the bowl is too large for the pan, it will move about too much – if it is too small it will hang too low in the pan. Cover the bottom of the pan with water, making sure the water does not touch the underside of the bowl. Bring to the boil and simmer gently.

2. Put the chocolate, water and golden syrup in the bowl and place it over the top of the simmering pan. Stir until the chocolate has melted and all the ingredients have blended together. Carefully remove the bowl from the pan and set aside.

3. When completely cool, stir in the single cream. Pour into a jug if using immediately, or store in the fridge for up to 2 weeks.

Ingredients

Makes 1 medium-sized jar

250g best-quality plain dark chocolate, broken into small pieces

6 tablespoons water

170g golden syrup

150g single cream

Ingredients

Makes approximately 400ml

3 egg yolks

60g caster sugar

25g plain white flour

1 vanilla pod

225ml milk

pinch of salt

Crème Pâtissière

Crème pâtissière is a delicious vanilla custard which is a perfect filling for Fresh Fruit Tartlets (see recipe p103) or profiteroles (see p72). Make sure it is cooked thoroughly, otherwise it will have an unpleasant taste of raw flour. Using a fresh vanilla pod gives a really intense vanilla flavour.

Method

1. In a bowl, beat together the egg yolks and sugar until thick and pale. Stir in the flour.

2. Slice open the vanilla pod and remove the small seeds with the blade of a knife. Place the milk in a heavy-based saucepan together with the salt and vanilla seeds and bring to the boil. Remove from the heat immediately.

3. Whisk the hot milk into the egg mixture, then return it to the pan. Place over a gentle heat, whisking the contents constantly until the custard is thick and smooth. If it should become lumpy at any stage, remove the pan from the heat and beat vigorously with a whisk until it becomes smooth again. The custard will keep for a couple of days in the fridge – cover the surface with cling film to prevent a skin forming.

Notes

Conversion Charts

WEIGHT			
Metric	**Imperial**	**Metric**	**Imperial**
5 g	⅙ oz	240 g	8½ oz
7-8 g	¼ oz	255 g	9 oz
15 g	½ oz	270 g	9½ oz
20 g	¾ oz	285 g	10 oz
30 g	1 oz	300 g	10½ oz
45 g	1½ oz	310 g	11 oz
55 g	2 oz	340 g	12 oz (¾ lb)
70 g	2½ oz	370 g	13 oz
85 g	3 oz	400 g	14 oz
100 g	3½ oz	425 g	15 oz
115 g	4 oz (¼ lb)	450 g	16 oz (1 lb)
125 g	4½ oz	510 g	1 lb 2 oz
140 g	5 oz	600 g	1 lb 5 oz
155 g	5½ oz	680 g	1½ lb
170 g	6 oz	700 g	1 lb 9 oz
185 g	6½ oz	800 g	1 lb 12 oz
200 g	7 oz	900 g	2 lb
215 g	7½ oz	1 kg	2 lb 4 oz
225 g	8 oz (½ lb)	1.35 kg	3 lb

VOLUME		
Imperial	**Metric**	**fl oz**
½ teaspoon	2.5 ml	1/12 fl oz
1 teaspoon	5 ml	⅙ fl oz
1 tablespoon	15 ml	½ fl oz
2 tablespoons	30 ml	1 fl oz
4 tablespoons	55 ml	2 fl oz
¼ pint (1 gill)	150 ml	5 fl oz
	225 ml	8 fl oz
½ pint	290 ml	10 fl oz
¾ pint	425 ml	15 fl oz
	450 ml	16 fl oz
1 pint	570 ml	20 fl oz
	900 ml	32 fl oz
2 pints	1.1 litres	40 fl oz
8 pints	4.5 litres	160 fl oz

LENGTH	
Metric	**Imperial**
0.5 cm	¼ inch
1 cm	½ inch
2.5 cm	1 inch
5 cm	2 inch
7.5 cm	3 inch
10 cm	4 inch
12.5 cm	5 inch
15 cm	6 inch
17.5 cm	7 inch
20 cm	8 inch
22.5 cm	9 inch
25 cm	10 inch
27.5 cm	11 inch
30 cm	12 inch

OVEN TEMPERATURES					
Aga/ Rayburn	**Gas mark**	**Electric °C**	**Aga/ Rayburn**	**Gas mark**	**Electric °C**
	¼	70°C		4	180°C
	¼	80°C	Fairly Hot	5	190°C
	¼	100°C	Hot	6	200°C
	½	110°C		7	220°C
Slow	1	130°C	Very Hot	8	230°C
	1	140°C		8	240°C
	2	150°C		9	250°C
Moderate	3	170°C		9	270°C

Index

These lists are not exhaustive, but you may find them helpful
when cooking for guests with special dietary needs.

Meat Free Recipes

Spring

Summer

Autumn

Winter

Gluten Free Recipes

Spring

Summer

Autumn

Winter